TOWARD A MORE
PERFECT FAITH

TOWARD A MORE PERFECT FAITH

4 Stages in Your Pursuit of God

A. W.
TOZER

Compiled by
Phil Shappard

MOODY PUBLISHERS
CHICAGO

Based on a sermon series preached by A. W. Tozer at Southside Alliance Church in Chicago, Illinois, January–March 1957. Transcribed and somewhat condensed from original audiotapes by Phil Shappard.

All Scripture quotations, unless otherwise indicated, are taken from the King James Version.

In chapter 2, one passage is quoted from *The Complete Bible: An American Translation,* J. M. Powis Smith and Edgar J. Goodspeed, trans. (University of Chicago, 1949), and one passage is quoted from *Rotherham's Emphasized Bible* (London: H. R. Allenson, 1902). In chapter 12, one passage is quoted from *Holy Bible from the Ancient Eastern Text: George M. Lamsa's Translations from the Aramaic of the Peshitta* (San Francisco: HarperSanFrancisco, 1933, 2014).

Compiled by Phil Shappard
Interior and cover design: Erik M. Peterson
Cover illustration of clouds © 2022 by sar14ev / Shutterstock (1388859272).
All rights reserved.

ISBN: 978-0-8024-3070-0

Originally delivered by fleets of horse-drawn wagons, the affordable paperbacks from D. L. Moody's publishing house resourced the church and served everyday people. Now, after more than 125 years of publishing and ministry, Moody Publishers' mission remains the same—even if our delivery systems have changed a bit. For more information on other books (and resources) created from a biblical perspective, go to www.moodypublishers .com or write to:

Moody Publishers
820 N. LaSalle Boulevard
Chicago, IL 60610

1 3 5 7 9 10 8 6 4 2

Printed in the United States of America

CONTENTS

INTRODUCTION

Devotional literature has a deep and expansive history going back over three thousand years. In it we experience the actual thoughts of people sharing their devotion to God. This may even make you think of a young shepherd boy worshiping his Creator while strumming a lyre under a starry sky as he kept watch over his family's sheep. His thoughts were a simple expression of love to God. He, like other early devotional writers, had little expectation their words would travel beyond their own environs, let alone their own lifetimes.

Such were possibly the thoughts of a man of God named Aiden Wilson Tozer, whose pastoral ministry spanned the early to mid-twentieth century. He was no ordinary Christian teacher, nor was his view of living out what he considered the normal Christian life. He believed those whom the Lord saved from sin were also called to live in victorious harmony, or communion, with God. So convinced of this, he often grew weary of Bible teachers who, as he believed, overemphasized their judicial relationship with God, often to the exclusion of teaching the abundant Christian life he felt was clearly revealed in the whole of Scripture.

As an example, he often decried the dangers of externalism, or what he called *living on the periphery*, trusting solely on embracing the correct words. He could trace its beginnings back to ancient Israel when "there came a slow shift from the center with God out toward the perimeter, out from the beating heart, out to the epidermis, out to the outside skin of things." He understood the propensity for the average Christian to live on the surface. He said, "Always men by centrifugal force tend to fly out to the outer edge of things, and always God through His prophets have urged men back to the center."

A. W. Tozer described externalism's dependence on words and ceremonies and forms. *Internalism*, on the other hand—that is, attention to personal spiritual growth—lies in content, in love, in worship, and in inward spiritual reality. He said God wants men to have content, but always men seek to be satisfied with words.

So he believed God sent prophets and seers and reformers, with whom he often related, to rebuke externalism. He well knew this stand didn't make him popular. His intense love of God, though, bid him no other option but to expose this form of fundamentalism that erroneously makes the Scriptures an end in itself, while the true intent of the Bible is to point Christians to the Author of the text, God Almighty.

Completely self-educated following his grade-school years, A. W. Tozer had a voracious appetite to read and learn. Books in the library transported him to the feet of many of the greatest sacred and secular writers. His common knowledge base was so steeped in ancient literature, poetry, and hymnody, he once mused the only subject he felt a little weak on was applied mathematics.

While Mr. Tozer didn't pastor a megachurch, he was in constant demand as a speaker throughout North America. The best description of his preaching style comes from one of his former associate pastors, Edward Maxey. He said it was like his writing; it had a poetic quality about it. His illustrations were often earthy and homey, mostly coming from country life and nature, but always singularly pointing to the truths found in Scripture.

Toward a More Perfect Faith follows in the same vein as Tozer's first devotional book, *The Pursuit of God* (1948), in which he seeks to reveal the person of God and man's attempts to know Him, simply because He could be found. Just as the fathers of modern science only attempted to discover natural physical laws due to their unwavering belief in a God who created an orderly universe, Tozer believed this same Creator made man solely in His image so they would become worshipers because He was a God who could not only be found, but known.

The basic premise of *Toward a More Perfect Faith* is the understanding that most followers of Christ live substandard Christian lives and need to be reminded that their profession of faith in Christ is not just an end unto itself. Tozer often preached that the faith once delivered was not to be merely accepted, but in fact was only a starting point for a life of graduated growth in consummate worship. A. W. Tozer believed this journey will take us through various stages of spiritual growth as described in the third chapter of the apostle Paul's letter to the church at Philippi. Intertwined with Paul's teaching, Mr. Tozer creatively brings his readers into a relationship with the writings of the anonymous author of the fourteenth-century devotional classic, *The Cloud of Unknowing*.

Rather than just an aggregation of compiled thoughts on spiritual growth, *Toward a More Perfect Faith* is the transcribed body of text taken from a series of twelve consecutive Sunday evening sermons A. W. Tozer preached from his Chicago pulpit between January and March of 1957. While edited to address a reading audience, great care was given to preserve his actual thoughts, allowing the integrity and fidelity of what he actually said to remain firmly intact. As you read this book, be prepared to learn new insights so you too can grow into a complete, or what has been called a perfect, Christian.

—PHIL SHAPPARD, compiler

THAT I MAY KNOW HIM, AND THE POWER OF
HIS RESURRECTION, AND THE FELLOWSHIP
OF HIS SUFFERINGS, BEING MADE
CONFORMABLE UNTO HIS DEATH.

—PHILIPPIANS 3:10

1

"ONED" WITH GOD

In Philippians 3:7–15 we find one of the most oft-quoted scriptural testimonies of a man who is desperately seeking after God. Yet, while reading this passage, you will find what seems to be a number of sharp contradictions in the writings of this man, the apostle Paul. That is, they only seem to be contradictory. Indeed, there is much in the teaching of Jesus that sounds contradictory. This can be said as well in the writings of the old saints and in their songs and in their hymns. They're not contradictory, though—they only seem to be.

In the Philippians 3 passage, the man Paul tells us we are not yet perfect, but then says, "as many as be perfect, be thus minded" (v. 15). This panting for perfection is the mood and temperature of the Law and the Psalms and the Prophets and the New Testament. It is also the temper of all the superior souls that have lived. It is these superior souls who have written our great books of devotion and have composed our loftiest hymns. We, the unworthy spiritual descendants of these great fathers, often sing these hymns and yet hardly know what we're singing.

I would like for one of these great souls to speak to us at times in this study ahead. Not to add to or take away anything from the Scriptures, but to illustrate and teach and devotionally expound. I am referring to the book *The Cloud of Unknowing*, which was anonymously written by an English author six hundred years ago. The writer states the purpose of his book is to help God's children grow spiritually and so go on to be what he calls "oned" with God. The book was written in pre-Elizabethan English and is older than Shakespeare by two hundred years, giving us some rather quaint language. There are more recent translations with modernized language, but I prefer the original text. The old writer who says he wants Christians to begin to be "oned" with God made a little prayer I would like to explain.

In the beginning of his little book of devotion, the old saint prays, "O God, unto whom all hearts be open, and unto whom all will speaketh." Let us notice that in his prayer he says that before God, all hearts be opened. That is, God can see in, even if you close your heart or lock it and have thrown away the key. Still, God can see in your heart as though it were standing wide open. And he continues, "unto whom all will speaketh." This is one of the doctrines of the Bible not heard of much today but very strongly emphasized in *The Cloud of Unknowing*, that the will of a man's heart is prayer.

"Prayer is the soul's sincere desire, uttered or unexpressed," wrote James Montgomery centuries later, though I suppose not borrowed from these writings we're looking at, considering he probably never heard of it. But "all will speaketh." In other words, what you will in your heart is eloquent, and God hears what you are willing, what you're determining to do, what you plan in your heart. *Unknowing* adds, "unto whom no privy thing is hid." That is, no secret thing is hid from God.

The anonymous writer then says, "I beseech Thee so for to cleanse the intent of my heart with the unspeakable gift of thy grace, that I may perfectly love Thee and worthily praise Thee." Some will worry about him using the word *perfect* as though he's pushing toward spiritual perfection. I would like to quickly counter that question with another. Is there anything wrong with the old saint's prayer? Can you find any theological fault with this prayer: "O God, fix my heart so I may perfectly love Thee and worthily praise Thee?" If this sounds extreme and fanatical to you, I would question your understanding of God's total salvation offered to you through Jesus Christ, for the true child of God will say an "amen" to this desire to perfectly love God and worthily to praise Him.

He goes on to say there are four stages in the Christian life. "I find four degrees and forms of Christian men's living," and names them: *common, special, singular,* and *perfect.* Those are the four stages. What an evangelist he would have made! Had he come around six hundred years later he would state, "Here's the way Christians are as I see them."

The first stage or form is the *common* Christian—God knows what a mob we are. Then there's the *special* Christian, one who has moved on a little, and then followed thirdly by the *singular* Christian. The final stage he lists is the *perfect* Christian. He then explains very carefully that the first three stages—common, special, and singular—may be commenced and ended in this life. The fourth stage, though, "may by grace be begun here, but it shall ever last without end in the bliss of heaven."

I would like to make it clear that neither I nor the writer of *The Cloud of Unknowing* are perfectionists to the point where we walk about with a benign St. Francis smile saying we're perfect. You will always find, though, there's a place to go on into deeper spiritual maturity, yet we both hold to the belief that you can at least enter into the beginning of spiritual perfection or completeness.

Along with this opening explanation I would like to offer a postulate, that is, something that is taken for granted that provides a basis upon which we may proceed. My postulate is the belief that most present-day Christians live beneath themselves and live sub-Christian lives. Most modern Christians are not joyful persons because they are not holy persons. They are not holy persons because they are not filled with the Holy Spirit. They're not filled with the Holy Spirit because they are not separated persons. The Spirit cannot fill whom He cannot separate. Whom He cannot fill, He cannot make holy; and whom He cannot make holy, He cannot make happy.

Stated differently, even though the modern Christian has been born again, having accepted Christ, often he's not a joyful person because he is not a holy person. And he's not a holy person because he's not filled with the Holy Spirit, the only Holy Spirit there is. He's not filled with the Holy Spirit because he's not separated from the world. God cannot fill what He cannot separate and He cannot make holy what He cannot fill. He cannot make joyful what He cannot make holy.

Furthermore, my postulate includes this: the modern Christian is not Christlike; that is, he has not been "oned" with Christ. The proof of this lies in the bad dispositional flaws found today among the children of God. If I didn't have prophetic vision to see down the years like the prophets in the eleventh chapter of Hebrews who fell asleep not having seen the fulfillment of the promise, I would be deeply despondent. The reality is, I have preached for years to some people who still have bad dispositional flaws. In addition to that, they have moral weaknesses, frequent defeats, and dulled understanding. They live outside the will of God and live beneath the Scriptures to a great degree, and thus outside the will of God. That is my postulate and the reason for this study.

This substandard condition is not too unfamiliar in the Bible. Remember what was written about Israel, God's people, in the Old Testament and often repeated in the New. Though the children of Israel should be as numerous as the sands by the seashore, yet but a remnant should be saved. Look at the fifth chapter of Hebrews where the writer says,

> Of whom we have many things to say, and hard to be uttered, seeing ye are dull of hearing. For when for the time ye ought to be teachers, ye have need that one teach you again which be the first principles of the oracles of God; and are become such as have need of milk, and not of strong meat. For every one that useth milk is unskilful in the word of righteousness: for he is a babe. But strong meat belongeth to them that are of full age, even those who by reason of use have their senses exercised to discern both good and evil. (Heb. 5:11–14)

That is only the beginnings of it, for he goes on:

Therefore leaving the principles of the doctrine of Christ, let us go on unto perfection; not laying again the foundation of repentance from dead works, and of faith toward God, of the doctrine of baptisms, and of laying on of hands, and of resurrection of the dead, and of eternal judgment. And this will we do, if God permit. (Heb. 6:1–3)

Our Lord also said the love of many would wax cold, for in the book of Revelation, in the seven letters to the churches found in chapters two and three, we have certain conditions laid out before us. These are churches that are functioning as churches but have lost their first love and are cold, and have very much wrong with them spiritually. Therefore, I have based the necessity for this study with the understanding most present-day Christians live sub-Christian lives. Unless you agree with my postulate, this may just be a waste of each other's time and a wasted effort on my part.

This study has cost me a tremendous amount of brainpower, nervous energy, and considerable spiritual preparation. It is one of the heaviest things that I know, to realize this teaching as well as the apostle Paul's text in Philippians 3 can mean nothing to some readers. In Matthew 13:10 and following, we read about the disciples who came and said unto Jesus,

Why speakest thou unto them in parables? He answered and said unto them, Because it is given unto you to know the mysteries of the kingdom of heaven, but to them it is not given. For whosoever hath, to him shall be given, and he shall have more abundance: but whosoever hath not, from him shall be taken away even that he hath. Therefore speak I to them in parables: because they seeing see not; and hearing they hear not, neither do they understand." (Matt. 13:10–13)

That very plainly states there were people who could not accept the teaching of Jesus. And so, in order that He might speak to the ones who could hear, He disguised His teaching a little bit. I don't mean He was deceiving, but He was fixing it with a kind of spiritual code so the ones who could get it, got it, and the others didn't get it. It was as though He was actually keeping it back from certain ones. We read the same thing by the man Paul in the third chapter of 1 Corinthians. He said, "I, brethren, could not speak unto you as unto spiritual, but as unto carnal, even as unto babes in Christ. I have fed you with milk, and not with meat: for hitherto ye were not able to bear it, neither yet now are ye able. For ye are yet carnal: for whereas, there is among you envying, and strife, and divisions, are ye not carnal, and walk as men? For while one saith, I am of Paul; and another, I am of Apollos; are ye not carnal? Who then is Paul, and who is Apollos, but ministers by whom ye believed, even as the Lord gave to every man?" (1 Cor. 3:1–5). He had to hold back certain truths because they couldn't receive it.

The anonymous writer of *The Cloud of Unknowing* admonishes everyone into whose hands his little book fell. He said,

I charge thee, and I beseech thee, in the name of the Father and of the Son and of the Holy Ghost, that thou neither read this book, nor write it, nor speak it, nor suffer it to be read, written or spoken of, or to any, excepteth it be such and one as have by true will, and by and of a whole intent, purposed him to be a perfect follower of Christ, not only in active living, but in the farthest point of contemplative living possible by grace, to become in this present life of a perfect soul yet in a mortal body.

What he is saying is, I don't want anybody bothering around with this unless you have made up your mind and have a true will and a whole intent and purpose in your heart to be a perfect follower of Christ.

Oh, believing friend, what has happened to us when we judge the intent of a man like this over against our nibbling in this modern time, when we must pull the preaching of the Word down to the level of the dumbest and most spiritually obtuse. Why is it we don't preach to the one who's really thirsting after God, but rather to the most *commonest* of Christians who barely hangs on. I hear *The Cloud of Unknowing* say to me, Tozer, by the grace of God and in the power of the Trinity, I beseech you, don't you preach this unless people are determined in their hearts to be perfect, or complete followers of Christ in the sovereign-est point of living possible by grace in this life.

When I hear the lyrics of a song that states, "His blood made us worthy," something leaps up in my heart causing me to say, "God, that's my hope; not me, but His blood has made us worthy." I hope by the blood of Jesus that we may be worthy to listen and, by the intent of our heart, perfectly to love God and worthily to praise Him. May we by grace follow Him in the most sovereign-est point possible in this life and get something out of this study.

The ancient writer goes on to mention he rejects certain people. He clearly states there are people he would consider rejects, those who disqualify themselves as potential readers. He states that among those he doesn't want to hear or read his book are the fleshly janglers, that is, idle-talkers or people that just chatter all the time. Nor does he want open-praisers and blamers of themselves and others to read his words. He also calls out the tellers of trifles and rowners. A *rowner* is a gossip. God knows them.

"O God, to whom no privy thing is hid and all will speaketh and all hearts are open . . . Thou knowest where the rowners are, the gossipers and the tattlers of tales," he said. You leave my book alone, you tale-tattlers and all manner of pinchers, he says. A pincher is the fellow who tithes, but whose hand holds on to his money as long as he can and pinches his money. The old writer says, "For mine intent was never to write such things unto them. Therefore, I would that they meddle not therewith; neither they, nor any of these curious, lettered, or unlearned men." If you're just a curious person in this deeper spiritual life teaching, whether you're ignorant or a scholar, it doesn't make any difference, he says. I don't want any of those people hearing what I have to say.

I have to contradict *The Cloud of Unknowing* on this point. I am not willing to withhold the open secret of spiritual power from those who can take it just because there are those who cannot. I am not going to withhold the open secret of the victorious life from those who can understand it because there are some present who cannot understand it. Jesus Christ told parables and disguised His teaching in order that the spiritual eyes might see it and so others will not see nor hear or understand. And so, through the course of this book, I have no doubt there will be a sorting out. There will be a sorting out with some willing to choose to go on in their devotion to Jesus Christ. Some will go on from stage to stage. Others will be content to remain as common Christians as we have in such great numbers in our day. Fundamentalism has unfortunately produced a whole herd or flock of common Christians in our day.

Further into our study I will discuss what it means to become a special Christian and define what kind of a Christian this is and then go on to discuss what it means to be a singular Christian. Please don't think I'm teaching about four works of grace. No one should think, "I've heard of two works of grace, and even some teach three, but Tozer's got four!" No, I'm just talking about four stages on the path toward spiritual perfection or maturity. Alongside our anchor teaching in Philippians 3, I want to also follow this man who says a man can be a common Christian in his life. He can also be a special Christian in his life and can even go on until he becomes singularly spiritual in his life. It is my prayer to also show it is possible for him to finish those three stages at the stage of perfection, and then move into a stage which you can only begin here, but you will never end, as the old writer says, "'til the bliss of heaven."

This is the teaching of the victorious Christian life and the focus of my teaching. As I continue, I am convinced there will be a sorting out. I could only wish this sorting out might come in religious circles. We've watered each other down so much until the solution is now so weak that if it contained poison, it wouldn't kill you, and if it were medicine, it wouldn't cure you. It is just a weak solution. This book is for those who want to go on unto the fullest measure, the sovereign-est point of living possible by grace to attain to in this present life while still living in this mortal body.

Is it fanatical to want to go on until you can perfectly love God, until you can perfectly praise God and thus live in the will of God so you are living in heaven while you're living on earth? If that is fanaticism, then it is the fanaticism of the Law. It is the fanaticism of the Psalms. It is the fanaticism of the Prophets and of the New Testament. It's the fanaticism that gave us Methodism. It's the fanaticism that gave us the Salvation Army. It's the fanaticism that caused the Christian and Missionary Alliance missionary society to be born. It's the fanaticism that gave us the Moravians. It's the fanaticism that gave us the Friends of God who held close to the truth. It's the fanaticism that caused the birth of the Reformation.

Let us remember these men who in times past were like worms in the soil, softening it up, getting it ready for the harvest. Unseen, but working in little groups here and there, were holy people that would not surrender themselves to the common ways of the world. Just as the angleworms and the other worms found in the soil, by their going through it and going through it, constantly keep the soil soft and making it so that when it rains the water can moisten it as is necessary.

Let me further illustrate by saying the plain saints, the simple saints, were not heard of much but lived lives of spiritual perfection, that is, at least the beginnings of spiritual perfection in this life. They salted down the nations like Germany and Holland and even the Latin countries until the Reformation came. They created a soft soil in which to plant the seed. Martin Luther could never have done what he did had there not been those before him. There were others like him who had gone up and down the land preaching such kind of living as this.

Some reading this will go on, and unfortunately some will not. Some will come to their Kadesh Barnea and turn back. When the people of Israel came to Kadesh Barnea, there were some who said, let's go on over, but Israel as a whole said no, we will not go over, and they didn't. So, they went back not knowing they were sentencing themselves to forty years of aimless wandering in the desert sands of the wilderness. They didn't know they were taking a test. God didn't say, "Now, stand up here everybody, take a deep breath, and we are going to be having a test." He simply let them make their own test—and they flunked it!

In this world of sin and flesh and devils, it's a frightening and terrible thing that about 80 to 90 percent of the people that God puts to the test flunk that test, but thankfully not all. Arise, O sleeper, and call upon thy God, if so be it that God will think upon us. I must say for some it will be an unconscious testing when we urge you forward. The question is, what is your response? Will you go this far with me? Will you agree that most Christians today live sub-Christian lives? Do you agree that most Christians are not joyful Christians? They're not joyful Christians because they're not spiritual Christians and, therefore, not holy Christians.

If your concept of Christianity is one of part play, part social fun, and part religion, you won't be able to hear or understand me at all. You may receive these words, but you'll never really understand what I am saying. On the other hand, if your concept of Christianity contains the belief that this life is a battlefield with this world, and this life is a preparation for something greater; if you accept the cross of Jesus Christ as your symbol which you must carry and die on it and rise and live above it, then we'll move along and we will have a good journey together.

I share with you now a little motto from *The Cloud of Unknowing*. It is this: "Look now forwards and let be backwards." This was the ancient writer's way of repeating what the apostle Paul said. Get rid of that backward path. Don't look back, but look now forward. If you will take that as your motto, "Look now forwards and let be backwards," and not worry about the past and commit to move forward through the successive stages, you will have a spiritual experience the old brethren called "oneness" with Christ. To be "oned" with Christ is what my own heart longs for, and I trust yours does as well.

2

STAGES OF GROWTH

When God speaks to us and we speak back to Him in prayer and devotion, what we say back to Him is very important. This is why the Psalms are so important, because in them we see inspired men speaking back to God. This is why the great devotional literature is so important. God speaks to us and the ages have spoken back to God, and God has preserved it for us.

I am following, albeit not too closely, some suggestions from the anonymously written book *The Cloud of Unknowing*. Its author addresses his readers as "ghostly friends," which is just an old word for a spiritual friend in God. "Thou shalt well understand that I find in my boisterous beholding, I find four degrees and forms of Christian men's living . . ." He states you can be a common Christian and then go on to be a special Christian and go on to be a singular Christian. And lastly, you can enter into the fourth stage, perfection, but you can't enter in fully because the fourth "may by grace be begun here, but it shall ever last without end in the bliss of heaven." This is a perfect response to what Paul said: "I count not myself to have apprehended: neither were already perfect: but let us therefore as many as be perfect, be thus minded." There is a blessed contradiction. We have entered in, but we haven't gone all the way yet.

What is this all about? Is this some weird, strange new thing that has been added? I think not. Here is what *The Cloud* says: "O God, unto whom all hearts be open and unto whom all will speaketh." That is, whatever you will, that's your prayer. Whatever you will, that is what's going up to God. God hears that. If you will to be evil, God hears that. If you will to be holy, God hears that. If you will to resist, God hears that. "All will speaketh and unto whom no privy thing is hidden," which means no private or secret thing is hid from God.

Can you find any fault with this? *The Cloud of Unknowing* further states, "I beseech Thee so for to cleanse the intent of my heart with the unspeakable gift of Thy grace that I may perfectly love Thee and worthily praise Thee." If that's fanaticism, then I, without any hesitation, say that I want to be that kind of fanatic. I too want my heart to be so cleansed by the unspeakable gift of the grace of God that I may perfectly love Him and worthily serve Him. Would you not like this to be your experience as well?

Proverbs 4:18 says, "The path of the just is as the shining light, that shineth more and more unto the perfect day." Here are two separate translations of that verse, the first of which is by Edgar J. Goodspeed: "The path of the righteous is like the light of the dawn that shines evermore brightly till the day is full." *Rotherham's Emphasized Bible* says, "The path of the righteous is like the light of the dawn, going on and brightening unto meridian day."

In the Old Testament man's inspired utterance, he clearly states when a Christian becomes a Christian, the sun comes out. The path of that Christian, as he moves along, is like the rising of the dawn and the growing of the day so that the light shineth more and more unto the perfect day. The Hebrew means, "until the sun stands still in heaven as it is up at the top, and the fullest day shall be yours." Christians often admire and quote this a great deal and even memorize it, but seldom believe it.

How do I know they don't believe it? Because most Christians simply do not experience it. And what we don't experience, we haven't believed. It is important to remember that most Christians remain right where they are, day after day and week after week, and the weeks go into months and the months go into years. Yes, we do have our little spells when we hope to do better. But if we are honest, most Christians remain where they are, day and month and year until old age creeps up on them. There are some who have not gone one inch further up the hill than when the sun first rose on their conversion. I'm not trying to de-convert them or unchurch them or say they're not a Christian. What I am saying is that they have stopped growing at the very point they should have started to advance in their knowledge of God.

You may ask, are not all Christians justified? Are not all regenerated? Are not all Christians members of the household of God and of the body of Christ? Why do you make distinctions between Christians? Are not all Christians saints, according to our Greek translations? Therefore, why should you make these distinctions, and why should you say there are common Christians, special Christians, singular Christians, and Christians that are beginning to mark perfection in their spiritual lives?

I've heard this line of spiritual reasoning for years that all Christians are alike and are without any distinction. I have fought it, resisted it, and argued about it for a long time and again ask, why did Christ in His parable of the sower in Matthew 13 talk of some thirty-, some sixty-, and some a hundred-fold in the Christian life? Why did He make a distinction? The Lord Jesus Himself described these. He said thirty, sixty, and a hundred. Why did Christ say that some should rule over many cities and some over a few cities? Why should some have high positions and some not so high in the kingdom of God?

Why did the apostle write the words in Philippians 3 if we're all alike and there's no reason to be disturbed at all? Why did he say he had suffered the loss of all things and counted them but dung that he might win Christ and be found in Him; and that he might know Him and the power of His resurrection and be conformable unto His death, and by any means he might attain unto that superior resurrection? Yes, Paul believed all Christians would be raised from the dead as Christians, but he spoke of a superior resurrection. As he said, "Not as though I had already attained, either were already perfect: but I follow after . . . forgetting those things which are behind."

Remember our little motto from *The Cloud of Unknowing*, "Look now forwards and let be backwards," which is early medieval or pre-Shakespearean English. We say to a child, "Let it be." It's an idiom for don't touch it, stop it, or quit. The ancient writer says let be backwards. Stop that backward look, and look now forward.

Let's now examine closer the word *common* or *ordinary*. We find its definition as of common rank or quality or ability. A common Christian is one who is of ordinary quality or ability and not distinguished by superiority of any kind. He is just a Christian who believes, but not distinguished by spiritual superiority of any kind. Good old *Webster's* says a common person follows customary ways. If you are simply a Christian of common quality or ability and not distinguished in any way, you are just following customary ways, whatever they may be. You are most likely a common Christian.

We now come to a word that I must confess I don't like. It's the word *mediocre*. The sad truth is, most Christians can be described as mediocre. Do you know what the word *mediocre* means? It comes from two Latin words meaning halfway up to the peak. I wonder if that doesn't aptly describe most Christians. They are halfway up to the peak. They are not halfway up to heaven, but halfway up to where they ought to be—halfway up the peak, halfway between the valley and the peak. They're not wallowing in the valley anymore, but they're not up to where the sun shines on the peak. They're morally above the hardened sinner, but they're spiritually beneath the shining saint. That's where most of us have now settled.

Maybe you have told yourself in the past you're not going to be mediocre because you hate that word also and decided to push your way up the mountain until you're at the top of the peak where you can be in this mortal life. Unfortunately, you've done nothing about it though. If anything, you lost a little ground. You're just a halfway Christian. I wonder if that is what Jesus meant when He said in Revelation 3, you're neither hot nor cold, but lukewarm. I wonder. I hope His words mean that, because I don't want to contradict myself by adding to the Scriptures.

Consider though what the word *lukewarm* means. I am not sure where the word *luke* originated, but we call it tepid now—water that is neither cold nor hot. It's just lukewarm, halfway up the peak, halfway up where you could have been if you had pressed on. If you turn and look back down the mountain and acknowledge you're not in the valley, down in the miasmic shadows and mist, but you're not where you could have been. That's what we call mediocre, morally above the hardened sinner, but spiritually beneath the adoring saint.

Understanding this, I must ask if this is the best that Christ offers, by His blood and His Spirit, by His hard dying on the cross, by His resurrection from the dead, by His ascension to the right hand of the Father, by His shedding forth of the Holy Spirit, by His inspiring the New Testament. Is a halfway Christian experience the best Jesus Christ offers? I wonder if He expects or accepts that we Christians should stop developing when we're half-grown. Do we honor God by stopping and freezing our development as if we were just fifteen, or do we honor God by going on to full maturity? Despite the clear teaching of the Bible, many of God's people tend to quit and arrest their development. Surely, that's not what the Lord wants. Mediocrity does not agree with the New Testament.

Have you ever considered why there are so many that can be called common Christians? It is because, even though we heard a call to take up the cross and follow toward the heights, we begin to bargain with God. Instead of going on, we began to ask questions. We began to dicker with God. I think this dickering with

God is one of the most hateful and one of the most repulsive things that I know in the religious and in the field of religion. As an evangelical conservative, I don't feel we should beat the heads off the poor liberal, because I don't think they're the ones that the Lord is worried about. He knows where they are spiritually. They're not Christians. But we who are Christians, who have been born again, we have life, and the root of the matter is in us. Yet, when the Lord calls us to the heights, we begin to dicker and we ask, what will it cost me? O Lord, I want to go on, but what will it cost me?

My friends, I hate to say this because it sounds brutal, but if anyone brings up the question of consequence in the Christian life, they are not a good Christian and are only a mediocre, common Christian, undistinguished by spiritual superiority in any phase of this life. Jesus told His disciples to take up their cross and follow Him, for where He was, they would be also; and if they did that, the Father would honor them.

So whoever takes up the cross never asks what the consequence is going to be, because everybody knows what the consequences of a cross are. As soon as we start dickering and question what it will cost me in time or money, we reveal to our own spirit we are a common Christian. I feel like I am even softening the edges of the sword of the Lord in what I am teaching. I think that I'm even making it easier than the Lord made it when He said those terrible, wonderful things about cross-carrying in the sixteenth chapter of Matthew.

Here's yet another question, and this is worse still—is it convenient? My God, how His work rests with the convenience of His people. To many, the work of the Lord is a convenience.

All advance in the Christian life must be made at our inconvenience. If it doesn't inconvenience you, there's no cross in it if you've reduced it to a smooth pattern and it costs you nothing. If there's no disturbance and no bother and not an element of sacrifice in it, you're getting nowhere. If you've stopped and pitched your unworthy tent halfway between the swamp and the peak, you're a mediocre Christian.

Have you ever heard of a cross that was convenient? Has anyone ever found a convenient way to die? If you wanted to die, and were a sinner and wanted to take your life, how would you do it? Is there any convenient way to die? I've never heard of any. Judgment will not be convenient, and yet we look around for convenience. Mountain climbers are always in peril and working at their inconvenience.

After first hearing the voice of Jesus speak to us and call us to Himself, would we ask Him if it will be fun? Anyone who asks this will only ever be a common Christian. He'll be mediocre until he dies. He'll never be distinguished in any way for any spiritual qualities. He'll never be outstanding for any gifts of the Holy Spirit. He'll never know the Lord more than the common rank and file. Christians who ask, is it fun? demand that Christianity be fun. Whole organizations have been started to give it to them. We have whole organizations dedicated to mixing religion and fun for our young people. Please understand, young people today are just as responsible before God as old people. The teenager who meets Jesus and is converted is just as responsible for inconvenience and cost as a man of seventy. There is no difference. And yet, we are seeking fun. Christ has never offered amusement and entertainment, yet we have to offer them both if we're going to get people because they are common Christians. It doesn't have to be that way.

Our fifth question is—is it popular? You say, "I'm a Christian. I have accepted Jesus; of course I have." We are talking about an advance now, of something ahead, something that's beyond the average. Is it common? Is it popular? Do other people do it? A Christian should never ask, is it popular? but should ask, is it the will of God?

Heaven is the place where the will of God is done. Hell is the place where the will of God is unknown except the judgment will that sent men there. And in between the heaven where the will of God is perfectly done, and the hell where it will never be done, is a group of people trying to make up their mind whether they want the will of God or not. When we say, is it popular? we are avoiding the pain of standing alone. Some people just can't stand alone.

I was converted at seventeen years of age. At the time, there was not a single Christian in my home. My mother had boarders in our home. My father was still alive, and the family along with my brothers and sisters were there. We had a house full of people all the time, yet I was alone. Alone. Alone. I know what Elijah meant when he said three times, O God, I am alone. I stood alone in that house. I don't want to give the impression that I stood as nobly as Stephen in Acts 7, but I did stand. It was tough standing alone with no one around me living as a Christian. No one to go to church with you. No one wanted to bow their heads and pray at the table. Nobody wanted a Bible. It was tough to stand alone, but by the good grace of God, I stood alone. The result was, my mother was converted, then my father, and then two of my sisters trusted Christ. My father was a Baptist and went to heaven. My mother was a Christian and died and went to heaven. Several others in my family were converted, but if I had said, "Lord, is it popular? What will it cost me?," those persons would have never met God. But by the grace of God, He did help.

Let's consider for a moment that maybe some have been guilty of asking these questions. Some who have accepted Christ as their Savior and know a change has come, yet may be asking themselves, "O God, if I seek You further, what will it cost me? O God, will it be safe for me to go on? O God, will it be convenient? Will there be any fun in it? Do I have to stand alone, God?" I have said it's ignoble. I have said it is unworthy. I have said it's the mark of mediocrity and the sign of commonness. You mustn't look back on your life and worry about it. Let us have confidence and let us not blame ourselves. When considering things like this, don't be bogged down by discouragement. Remember our motto, "Look now forwards and let be backwards."

Think for a moment if you were to be stopped spiritually where you are right now and are nailed to a rock like Prometheus was when they bound him on the rock for stealing fire from heaven. Are you going to be nailed to a rock halfway up the peak? Prometheus was an old Greek god who was like a chameleon who could take the shape of whatever he wanted to be. He could take any shape. In snow he could be white, and in the coal mine he could turn black. He was a changeable god. Of course, he was no God. Paul says there isn't any, but we're illustrating as Paul himself did.

Pride is like that too. Pride is a devilish thing. Pride changes color wherever it may be. If it's a liberal church, it wears white gloves and looks out with pride on the many judges and senators that belong to the church. If it is a fundamentalist church, it changes color and smugly smirks about its evangelical doctrine and its belief in the verbal inspiration of the King James Version. If it is a deeper life church like ours, it changes its color again. Christians who have gone on to seek a deeper walk with the Lord are often tempted to be proud of it. Those who haven't are tempted to be discouraged about it. Remember, pride is a devilish thing.

I have attempted to lay before you my understanding of a common Christian from my many decades of ministry, prayer, and Bible study. If you are discouraged by these descriptions of a common Christian, I ask you not to be discouraged. That's pride. What's happening to you now is you're ashamed of the way you live. You were so proud of yourself, but when you hear or you see yourself exposed, you naturally feel ashamed of yourself. This is just pride. You have to stop thinking about yourself without worrying, and look now forwards and let be backwards.

What are in the "backwards" of your life? Can we not trust that the Lord will take care of all that? He pardons instantly and forgives by the forgiving love of God and the restoration of restored innocence and the blood of the Lamb and the worthiness His blood gives. His blood makes us worthy. With all my heart, I want to underscore the words of the simple song, His blood makes us worthy. If you go back and beat yourself like the flagellants and whip yourself until you bleed, and go about showing how spiritual you are by confessing that you've been no good, you will simply be fussing with yourself. Stop fussing with yourself. Stop it and look now forward. No one will ever go any distance until he gets his eyes up and stops looking at himself.

The human's eyes were made to look out, not in. God meant for you and me to look out, not back in. Introspection is a long word which just means what it says—*spect*, from *spectro*, meaning "I see," and *intro*, from the in. So, we have looked in the in. But there's another word and that's *prospect*, and that means looking forward. And so, let's not look back.

Believing friend, if you want to move forward, you'll never make any progress by going back and digging up everything that's wrong with you. It's like the story of dragon's teeth that were sown in the ground and every tooth became a dragon. The more you dig in it at yourself, the more you'll harm yourself. It's like operating on yourself. You can dig at yourself and condemn yourself and wallow in your own self-accusation until you have forgotten all about the blood and all about the good grace of God. It must start right now, exactly where you are. "Lo, He maketh all things new." He is the God of new beginnings. Look now forwards, and let be backwards.

We can rejoice for the old times are gone under the shed blood of Jesus Christ. A quick, sincere word to the Lord that you're sorry for the way you've been well taken care of, and the Lord will let it fall from you as the burden rolled from Christian in *The Pilgrim's Progress* and rolled down the mountainside. From there on, it will be forwards and not backwards. If you keep looking back at the mistakes you've made and back on the sins you've committed and back at your ignoble mediocrity and back at how common you've been and how undistinguished your spiritual life has been, it will nail you to a rock halfway up the hill.

So the thing to do is stop blaming yourself. While we often find it quite easy to get victory over our humility, it's not so easy to get victory over our repentance and victory over the constant blaming of ourselves. Let's not blame ourselves. He knoweth our frame. If you were to take yourself apart until every grain of dust out of which you're made was lying dry before the eyes of God, you wouldn't tell God anything. He knows you are dust. And if you go back into your life and dig up everything that memory would help you to dig up, you wouldn't tell God anything. God already knows all about that. He knoweth our frame. He remembers that we are dust. Oh, that sweet 103rd Psalm. I thank God it was ever written. He knoweth our frame. "Like as a father pitieth his children, so the LORD pitieth them that fear Him," for He knows our frame. He remembers that we are dust.

So that's an extended look at the makeup of a common Christian. I've tried my best to describe him. I have given you a number of reasons why he is like that. I will now move on to tell you what the common Christian can do about his predicament. I will move on to talk about the special Christian; that is, one who has passed out of the state of mediocrity and is no longer nailed to a rock. He is loosed and he's traveling. As our old friend, six hundred years with the Lord from *The Cloud of Unknowing*, says, look now forwards and let be backwards!

3

INTERNALS OVER EXTERNALS

We've considered the first stage in the maturity of Christian believers by examining what we have called the common Christian. Common Christians as a whole are undistinguished by any marks of spiritual superiority. As first introduced to us in the six-hundred-year-old book *The Cloud of Unknowing*, I mentioned this was a characteristic of most of us common Christians. Establishing this, I believe we should all press forward to at least become a special kind of Christian.

Please take note of this man Paul in Philippians 3. This strange man Paul. This master of logic, who could escape logic and fly away from it as a bird escapes the birdcage when the door is left open. He said, "that I may win Christ." And he said this in a tense voice, "that I may win Christ," and yet he already had Him. That I may win Him and yet already have Him. He said, that I may be "found in Him," and yet he was already in Him. And it's to Paul that we look to more than any other writer in the

Bible to learn the doctrine of being in Christ. Yet Paul says that I may be "found in Him" when he was already in Him; "that I may know Him," when he already knew Him. He could testify, "I am crucified with Christ: nevertheless I live; yet not I, but Christ liveth in me: and the life which I now live in the flesh I live by the faith of the Son of God, who loved me, and gave himself for me" (Gal. 2:20). He went on to say in Philippians 3:14 that he followed after and pressed toward the mark and yet had not attained; he was trying to apprehend, that is, lay hold of that for which Christ had laid hold of him.

Notice how utterly foreign this is to the spirit of modern orthodoxy. "That I may," that blazing expression of the man Paul. "That I may" has been displaced by the words "I have." I have—because we can quote the text, we assume that we have the experience. This is to my mind one of the gravest hindrances to spiritual progress and one of the deadliest, most chilling breezes that ever blew across the church of God. This strange textualism that assumes that because we can quote the verse, therefore we have the content of the verse. I can walk around the First National Bank, but I don't own one red penny in the First National Bank. I can look out upon and memorize and yet not have one of the things that I've memorized in the Scripture.

"That I may"—those were the words that drove Paul. But now we are told, "I have." You are in Christ—be thankful. You have Christ—be thankful. Go on to cultivate. One of these times He'll come, and then you will see what you now have. I say that they are foreign to each other. They do not belong together. The yearning and panting language of the man Paul, who, like the roe who pants after the water brook, so panteth his soul after

Thee, O God. We are a stranger to this kind of thing. We study it in the Greek and we find out what it means in English, and then we say, isn't that fine now? Isn't that fine? And that's about all we do about it.

But Paul said, "I press toward the mark for the prize of the high calling of God in Christ Jesus" (Phil. 3:14). Now some have *wussified* that, meaning they have turned that into a pink cloud that they're going to get in the end. They believe that Paul meant a pink cloud out there that he was going to get when Christ returned. There's nothing here about Christ returning that I can see in that verse. It is a present effort to apprehend experientially that for which Christ apprehended him.

Unfortunately, there are some who can't hear what I'm saying. There are some who can't take this teaching and thereby possibly move on. I know it. But I know people, and I know there may be others who will listen and respond. There are some, though, who just can't hear what I'm talking about because they have been stopped dead by what I have called the creed of contentment. You are complete in Him. Be glad, therefore. You're complete and there's nothing else that can be done for you. In this rationale, it is felt that any effort to go ahead is considered to be some sort of fanaticism. So, over the past years the New Testament, particularly the book of Romans, has been so expounded. If there was such a word meaning "badly expounded" or "now expounded," I'd use it. It has been so expounded to stop us dead in our forward motion.

There are also others who just cannot hear this because they have met some truth for which they will not obey. Be assured, the Lord will positively not quibble over any truth that you won't obey. If you will not obey it, or if you stop somewhere because there is something you won't do, something that you refuse to do, some confession you won't make, some straightening out that you won't do, some act of obedience you won't perform, then you have been brought to a dead halt. That's just like a breaking of an axle on a truck or a car. It's a dead halt. There's no going on from there. And there are people like this sitting all around in the church of Christ who are saved. You can't say they're not saved. They have trusted Christ. They do believe their sins are forgiven. They do testify to being Christians, but they have a broken axle and haven't made one mile's progress in twenty-five years. Many people have heard good preaching over the years and yet sit with that broken axle, absolutely stopped dead by non-obedience.

Then, there are many who just can't hear what I'm saying because they have accepted a state of chronic discouragement as the normal condition for a Christian. They are believers, but they're not believers for themselves. They say they believe for others, but for them there's just no use. I've been to every altar. I have attended the Bible conferences. I've gone everywhere and I believe in this life, this progressive, victorious Christian life, but it can't be for me. So, they get into a state of chronic discouragement.

Here is what discouragement or unbelief says, because it's about the same thing. It says yes, I believe what you are preaching for somebody else, but not for me. Some other time, but not now. Some other place, but not here. That's supposed to be modesty and meekness, but it is neither modesty nor meekness. It is discouragement resulting from unbelief. We believe it is possible to accept there was a man who lived six hundred years ago in England who could talk about *The Cloud of Unknowing*, but we don't believe that there is such a thing now. We believe for that man, but not for us; for that time, but not for now; for that place, but not for here. So I say there are some who are discouraged. They have a chronic state of discouragement like someone who has been sick for so long and no longer believes they themselves can get well.

Do you remember when Jesus saw the man lying by the gate at the Pool of Bethesda? He said, "Wilt thou be made whole?" (John 5:6). Why did Jesus say that to that man? He never said that to anyone else in the New Testament. Wouldst thou want to be made whole? Why did He ask that man, Do you want to be made whole? Shouldn't any sick person want to be made well? Only up to a given point is that true. Only up to a given point does the average man or woman want to get well. It is possible that after they have lived with a chronic illness long enough, it becomes a pet they don't want to lose, because they wouldn't have any subjective conversation after that. They sort of feel that they are martyrs, and they pity themselves and feel that's their cross to bear and don't want to get well. They've learned to live with a low-grade, chronic sickness. If it's a roaring fire of sickness, of course, they're scared, but if they've had it for twenty years and it hasn't killed them, they figure they can last twenty more, so they don't try to get well. "Wilt thou be made whole?" He said, and then He made him whole because he wanted to be made whole. If He had found in that man what we Christians have in most of us—a chronic state of discouragement—He would have passed him by.

There's another reason why a lot of people can't hear what

I'm teaching. It's because they have accepted the cult of respect-ability. I have wanted to write about this just so I can get it out of my system, because I see the cult of respectability in religious circles. We have chosen to be cool and proper and poised and self-possessed and well-rounded. The word we use now is *adjusted*. We have learned to be adjusted. It's as though everybody is rushing at you with a screwdriver and trying to adjust you. We go to school to get adjusted. That is, we think we ought to become adjusted. They introduce psychiatric schools of thought into the church, where hired men come in with their screwdrivers and adjust people. So it is that everyone wants to be adjusted.

No one wants to be thought to be extreme on anything. Everybody wants to be well-rounded, properly adjusted, broad, symmetrical, and well-poised. We Christians get that way, forgetting that every superior soul, from Christ on, was at first considered extreme and even deranged. We sing brothers Charles and John Wesley's hymns and talk about them as if they were saints, which indeed they were. But do you know that when John Wesley lived, he couldn't keep a decent suit of clothes on because of the eggs that were thrown at him? Methodists today would drop dead if they realized their society's founder—a learned, Oxford man—was such a fiery apostle that people used to throw eggs and rocks at him, leaving him all banged up from preaching a sermon. He was considered to be a little off, and so was almost everyone else that has ever made any spiritual progress.

This idea of keeping cool and proper and poised and self-possessed and well-adjusted to society and symmetrically developed in all of our proper spheres of living is just a cult of respectability. No one wants to be thought extreme, and no one wants to be taught extremes in religion, so we often get converted and stop right there at the beginning. Thank God, though, there are a few that the Bible speaks of who are considered worthy. In Revelations 3:4 we read, "They shall walk with me in white: for they are worthy." I don't know what He meant exactly, but I know there are some people such as this. Even in the time of backsliding and general coldness of heart, there were some people who were different and were sufficiently different in that it was said of them that they walked with Him in white, and they were worthy.

I'm not trying to whip up desire for the simple reason that I know better. I know I can't whip up desire in your heart. I may be able to irritate you mentally or agitate you nervously, but I can't put desire in your heart. Listen to the words of the old writer from six hundred years ago with his quaint language. He says, "Our Lord hath of His great mercy called thee and led thee unto Him." Now, are you prepared to say that our Lord, of His great mercy, has called thee and led thee unto Him? How? By the desire of thine heart. It is He that put that desire in there. God is always previous. I wrote those little words one time, quoting somebody else, and it has now become quite a little phrase. God is always previous. God is always there first. So, this man knew that our Lord hath of His great mercy done this, and if you have any desire after God, God first put it in your heart.

The Cloud of Unknowing goes on to state, "When thou wert living in the common degree of Christian men's living, in the company of thy worldly friends. At that time, through the everlasting love of His Godhead, through the which He made thee and wrought thee when thou wert nought." Do you remember when you were not? I don't remember when I was not. Through the everlasting love of His Godhead, He made us and wrought us when we were not.

Let's settle this. God was there previous. You didn't call up. No one has a special telephone line to heaven, because you were not. You weren't even an idea yet. And yet God, through the everlasting love of His Godhead, made you when you were not, and then He bought you with the price of His precious blood when you are lost in Adam. Again, He preceded you. God was previous once more. I believe in prevenient grace, but I don't believe that a person can ever be nudged or pushed or jostled into the deeper life or into the kingdom of God except the Holy Spirit does it. God has got to be there previous.

So God bought you with the price of His precious blood. He made you when you were just a zero. He put legs on you and arms and a head and a heart and made you a human being and breathed into you the breath of life, and you became a living soul when you were nothing but a zero, out in vacuity and emptiness. He did that out of the everlasting love of His Godhead. Do you know that the more I teach about this, the bigger the sea of glory I see we Christians are in?

Then *The Cloud* says when you were lost in Adam, He bought you with a price, and goes on to say so tenderly, "He would not suffer thee to be so far from Him." He just wouldn't allow it. He just couldn't stand it. This same God that made you when you were nothing and redeemed you when you had sinned, He might not suffer thee to be so far from Him in form and degree of living. Therefore, "He kindled thy desire full graciously." Does that describe you? Have you ever had a sudden kindling of desire full graciously when everybody else around you seemed contented with panel discussions and how to build new buildings?

I recently read a magazine with articles on how to build a church. They spelled out the best techniques, such as to be careful where you locate. There were articles on how others did it with cautions where you should locate and how you can build on a small budget. Unfortunately, everything about this church had to do with externals. There wasn't one heartbeat in the whole thing, not a single heartbeat in the whole thing! We often live like that, and then one day suddenly He "kindle[s] thy desire full graciously, and fasten[s] by it a leash of longing." The picture of God leading a lamb down the street on a little leash—He fastened it with a leash of longing. The old writer said, "He kindled thy desire . . . and fastened by it a leash of longing." Notice how we see a fellow with a fire and he's leading that fire. He's leading that fire on a leash.

In light of God always being previous, I would like to point out the obvious trouble with logic. The trouble with logic is, it's no good. The truth about logic is that it will always bind you somewhere. To the man who sees God, logic just goes tumbling in all directions. Paul says, I know Him and I want to know Him. I have Him and I want to have Him. He's in me, and yet I'm seeking after Him. What are you talking about, Paul? He said, I know logic suffers there, but this is spirituality.

And so, here's a man who says, when you were nothing, God made you, and when you were a sinner, He redeemed you. Then, after you were wallowing around in a common kind of living, He "kindled" in thee most graciously a full desire, the fire of longing, and then fastened it by leash. I can't completely explain this. It doesn't bother me at all that this man is mixed up in his figures of speech by describing a man going down the street leading a fire on a leash, yet that's what God did for this man. He said, you were a common Christian. You didn't have a distinguishing feature about you. You didn't have anything that marked you as a Christian. You're just one more, and then there came that full gracious desire and that flame of longing into your heart. And God fastened it there to lead you by it into a more special state and form of living to be a servant among the special servants of God.

You must understand, there is no pride in this. How could there be any pride in this when the old writer says and Paul says and they all say and I try to say that there's nothing that any of us did, but God did the whole thing? You might as well try to create yourself as to try to redeem yourself. You can't do either one. And so, you might as well try to redeem yourself as to try to get any longing in your heart. It has to come from God, and if it doesn't come from God, and if you're bogged down somewhere, there's nothing I know to do. If you're stopped by the creed of contentment, if you've met truth and you won't obey, if you've accepted the chronic state of discouragement as normal, if you would rather be respectable than to be spiritual, I can't do anything for you, because I can't put any longing in you. I can't do it.

When I was a young man, I traveled down south and used to ride the old Vicksburg and Pacific Railroad selling peanuts, popcorn, chewing gum, and candy, as well as books. I eventually quit because I usually just sat and read the books while traveling from Vicksburg to the end of the line and hardly sold anything.

I do remember one thing, though. We used to go down through the day coach and give each person four or five kernels of salted peanuts. No one wanted any when you first went down the aisle, but on our return trip, everybody wanted more because they had gotten a taste of the salt and the peanuts, and they all wanted a bag. I can't do that for you here. That is just impossible. I can't make you long after God. If you don't have a longing after God and have accepted a common state of spiritual living and have no yearning, God hasn't kindled it in you full graciously—kindled in you a desire and fastened it with a leash of love. All you can do is just go ahead and hang on the Greek text and hope to get to heaven by a miracle.

Now, I want you to notice that all the spiritual adventures were internal before they were external. They were inside before they could be outside. This fire of desire, this leash of longing, this desire to prospect the hills of God for new loads of gold was all inward before it could be outward, and the outward was only secondary. If you were to study Abraham or study any of these men that I have mentioned or any of your heroes through the years, you will find it all happened inside them before it happened outside. Something had to happen within before there was any change on the outside. You can make every kind of change on the outside and yet not experience the change that touches the heart on the inside. It's at least technically possible to be a missionary and go to the field and spend a lifetime there, yet never have moved out of your little patch of ground in your own spiritual life. It is perfectly possible.

A retired missionary once came and knelt at the altar where I was preaching. At first, I was hesitant to go to him because I had just honored him. He was an old missionary who had spent a lifetime on the field in Africa. I finally did go to him and ask him, "What do you want, brother?" He said, "Brother Tozer, you know me. I have spent a lifetime as a missionary, but I have never been filled with the Holy Ghost. I know nothing about it. I've never been a Spirit-filled Christian." This man went out on the field in his body, but he didn't make the journey in his soul. I am not pleading for you to make a journey on your feet. You can go around the world and back. You can go among the aborigines and the stone-age Dani people and still never make the journey in your heart. This is a journey for the heart, not a journey for the feet.

For those who want to go on to a closer walk with God—and will go on—I want to mention a little bit more of what *The Cloud of Unknowing* said many years ago. He said, "Look up now, weak wretch, and see what thou art. What art thou, and what has thou merited, thus to be called of our Lord?" What are you and what have you got and what have you merited, he says, thus to be called by our Lord? "What weary wretched heart, and sleeping in sloth, is that the which is not wakened with the draught of this love and the voice of this calling?" How long have you been a common Christian and just like other people, measuring yourself by others and judging yourself by others and thanking the Lord you're converted? And here you are, a weak wretch, sleeping in your sloth, and you have never been wakened by the draft of His love nor the voice of His calling.

Some hear His voice; I'm quite sure of it. You need not worry; it won't lead you astray. You have your Bible. Some people would have to go a long way before even remotely being anywhere dangerously fanatical. The ancient writer continues, "Thou shouldest just be more meek and loving unto thy spiritual spouse, that He that is the Almighty God, King of kings and Lord of lords, who would meek Him so low unto thee and amongst all the flock of His sheep so graciously would choose thee to be one of His specials."

If God has laid something on your heart, or a longing to migrate, a longing to get up and say, "God, if You will lead me by the Scriptures and the Spirit, I'll go forward. I've hung around here and heard You say, 'You've dwelt long enough in this place. Get thee up and go into a land which I will show thee'"—if you have heard that, God has graciously called you and chosen you to be one of these specials. And then, "set thee in the place of pasture, where thou mayest be fed with the sweetness of His love." Some of God's dear children aren't in the place of pasture. If they get a longing, it dies after the first sermon they hear or after the first song they hear because no one has prepared them. God has not only called you, but He puts you where you get a place of pasture, and He does it all by the sweetness of His love. And then that passage comes, "look now forwards and let be backwards and see what thou lackest and not what thou hast."

Years ago, I was studying other religions like that of the Hindu, Buddhism, and Zoroastrianism religions and various religions of the East. As I was reading about the Upanishads, the writings of the Hindus, I came upon a passage that I thought was pretty cute. It says, any of you students who are busy learning texts and not living them, you're like a man counting other people's cattle who has not one heifer of his own. I would translate that by saying there are a lot of people doing that today.

They're counting other people's cattle. They're learning theology and eschatology and all the other ologies, but they haven't got one little horny heifer of their own. They only have something that belongs to someone else. Now he says, "See what thou lackest and not what thou hast." Don't start counting what you have in Christ, but start wondering what you have in yourself. The problem the church faces today is to get that which we have in Christ into us. It's a problem we in the church do very little about.

He now says, if you're going to do anything about this, and if you're going to forget what is past and look forward as the apostle Paul said, look now forwards and let be backwards. You are going to have to start dealing with where you haven't been and not where you have been. Don't trumpet what God has done for you. Look at what He hasn't done yet for you because you wouldn't let Him. *The Cloud* says, "All right from here, on all thy life now, all together must stand in desire. This desire behoveth all together be wrought in thy will by the hand of Almighty God and thy consent." He's saying, from here on, instead of easing back and taking it easy, you're going to look to God for a longing desire for Him such as Paul had and such as this man had, such as Faber had, such as Fénelon had and Samuel Rutherford and all the great and superior souls. "All thy life now behoveth to stand in desire."

He goes on to say, "If thou shalt profit in degree of perfection" with this desire coming to you by the hand of God and your consent. Do you know why we have not the desire? It's because we won't let God give it to us. It comes to you by the hand of God and our consent. God says, here, I'm ready to pour a little liquid fire into your heart. And we say, "No, God, excuse me, that would make me strange. I'd be fanatical. Besides that, I'd have to give up some things," and we just won't let Him. We want His heaven and we want the benefits of His cross and we want the bridge over hell, but we won't let Him kindle the love of our desire. He says if you've got any desire, it's got to come by the hand of God and by your consent.

The ancient writer shares an additional thought. It is a beautiful thing. He says, "He wills, thou do but look on Him and let Him alone." Do you understand this? Look on God and let Him alone. If you will just let God alone and stop stopping Him and quit preventing Him, God will kindle your heart and bless you and lead you on out of the common state where most everyone is into a state of special longing after Him for your spiritual life. He will begin to kindle like the rising sun, for the path of the just is as the shining light that's brighter more unto the perfect day. If you will work along with Him, any longing you have comes from God. Don't forget that. It isn't yours and you have no right to claim it. If you don't have it, it's because you won't let Him, for He puts it in your heart by His hand and your consent. And after that, "He wills thou do but look on Him and let Him alone."

He closes one of his writings, and I now close mine for the moment, with these words: "Press on then and let's see how you bear it. God is full ready." You don't have to coax God. Isn't that wonderful to know? We don't have to get on our knees and coax God and beg Him like a reluctant father is begged by his child. He's ready; He says He's ready. He does but abide thee, and all you have to do is press on and He's full ready. And He doth but abide thee. He wills thou but look on Him and let Him alone.

This looking on God and letting Him alone isn't the modern way most Christians think. We think God does the hard work and He's glad to have us along to help out. But he says, "Look on God and let Him alone." Get your hands down to your sides and stop trying to tell God where to operate. Stop trying to tell God where to rub. Stop trying to tell God what to give you. He's the Physician and you're the patient. Look on Him and let Him alone. This is wonderful doctrine.

Everybody talked about A. B. Simpson. They didn't always go along with him. He was thought to be a little bit off, but they were glad to sneak his books in and read them because he said we should let God work. The apostle Paul believed it when he said, "For it is God which worketh in you" (Phil. 2:13). Look on Him and let Him alone.

4

DISCOVERING CHRIST HIMSELF

Even though I have been basing my teaching on the third chapter of Philippians, I am also allowing the unknown author of the six-hundred-year-old book *The Cloud of Unknowing* to help us a little along the way. From this ancient spiritual literature, I have pulled out two mottos for spiritual growth. The first one was: "Look now forwards and let be backwards." This seems to be understood by most people. The second motto I stated was: "He wills thou do but look on Him and let Him alone." I would like now to give you an additional saying worthy of your attention: "He is a jealous Lover, and He suffereth no rivals."

I have mentioned there are four identifiable stages a Christian might attain in his or her spiritual journey. The first stage can be described simply as the common Christian, about which I have already written. I would like to share some additional thoughts about the stage called the "special Christian" which I introduced in the previous chapter. In future chapters, we'll examine what our unidentified writer called the "singular Christian." And finally, there is a fourth stage in which the Christian has moved up into God until he has begun to be perfect or thoroughly complete. Paul, as well as the old writer, believed that while we may begin this fourth state on earth, the life of perfection or spiritual completeness will not be fully realized until we attain it in the bliss of heaven.

The apostle Paul is our example. He states his desire—that I may know Him. The word *know* found in the tenth verse means acquaint or acquaintance. It also means experience. It means these two things, to be acquainted with and to have experienced. It is possible for you to be acquainted with a man and yet not have experienced the man in any sense of the word. For instance, if I introduce you to a friend, you could say you are acquainted with him, yet you have not experienced him in the sense that I have. I have traveled with him, preached with him, prayed with him, and spent endless hours talking with him. There's a difference between acquaintance and experience.

To get acquainted with God is one thing, but to go on to experience God in intensity and richness of acquaintance is something more. Paul said he wanted to know Him in that depth and rich intensity of experience because, as I have often said, personality can't be fully known with just one encounter. You may meet a person you don't particularly like at first, but after you get to know them, you begin to like them as you find the hidden potentialities in their personality that you were first unaware of.

Christians need to understand they possess the capability to have an increasing intimacy of acquaintance with Christ. One of our greatest weaknesses in the evangelical church of Christ is not that we don't know Christ in a rich intimacy of acquaintance; we're not even talking about it. We don't even hear about it. It is not to be found in most of our media today. Worse yet, this yearning, this longing to know Him in increasing measure is not found in our churches today.

I would like to point out that we can indeed enjoy an ever-increasing acquaintance with *That*. I want you to understand my use of the word *That*. You say, "But Jesus Christ is a *He*, a person. Why do you call Him 'That?'" You may not understand this now, but as Paul says, "If you think otherwise, God will reveal even that unto you." Before we can know God as a Him, we must know God as That. I think every theologian would agree with me on that. We find in the book of John what was said to the Virgin Mary: "*That holy thing which is born of thee shall be called the Son of God.*" That holy thing which is born of thee.

John was not an amateur theologian. This man who had laid his head upon the breast of Jesus begins his wondrous first epistle with the word *that*: "That which was from the beginning, which we have heard, which we have seen with our eyes, which we have looked upon, and our hands have handled, of the Word of life" (1 John 1:1). Personality is not found there yet. "For the life was manifested, and we have seen it, and bear witness, and shew unto you that eternal life, which was with the Father, and was manifested unto us; that which we have seen and heard declare we unto you, that ye also may have fellowship with us; and truly our fellowship is with the Father, and with His Son Jesus Christ" (1 John 1:2–3). It's not until the last two lines of the third stanza that he puts personality in there—it's "that" before.

Remember, Jesus Christ is a person. He is the Son, the eternal Son. He is also that which is the source of everything. He is the foundation and fountain of everything you and I are created to enjoy. He is the fountain of all truth, but He is more. He is truth itself. He is the source and spring of all beauty, but He is beauty itself. He is the fountain of all wisdom, but He is more. He is wisdom itself, and in Him are all the treasures of wisdom and knowledge hidden away. He is the fountain of all grace. He is the fountain and source of all life. But He is more than that. He said, I am the Bread of Life and I am the Life. He is the fountain of love. But He is more than that. He is Love. He is the resurrection, and He is immortality. And He is, as the song says, "brightness of my Father's glory, sunshine of my Father's face."

In light of who He is, we must now consider who we are and seek to understand the source of our often-weak spiritual condition. It is important for us to try to discover what is wrong with us when we start to backslide in groups and denominations and churches and as individuals. I believe our Lord Jesus hit the head of it when He said ye have left your first degree of love. Not your first love consecutively in the sense that there's love number one, love number two, and love number three, but He said you left your first degree of love. My entire preaching ministry has been trying to bring about in the church of Jesus Christ a rediscovery of the loveliness of the Savior that we might begin to love Him again with an intensity of love such as our fathers knew. I have said many times, the power and greatness of A. B. Simpson was not in his theology, but it lay in his unquenchable love for the person of Jesus Christ the Lord.

There are two stanzas in the song "Fairest Lord Jesus" that we often fail to appreciate. The first one says,

> *Fairest Lord Jesus, ruler of all nature*
> *O thou of God and man, the Son.*
> *Thee will I cherish, Thee will I honor.*
> *Thou, my soul's glory, joy, and crown.*

We know that one and two others, but there are other stanzas that we don't fully understand. One of them says,

> *Fair are the flowers. Fairer are its children*
> *When viewed in youth's unclouded day.*
> *Yet they must perish, all will soon vanish.*
> *Jesus alone abides for aye.*

Gaze out upon the world, on your family, your friends, your loved ones, all the lovely beauty of children and young people viewed in earth's unclouded day. Yet, candor and realism compel us to say, yet they must perish. All will soon vanish. And when they have vanished, we have only Jesus who alone abides for aye.

Another verse says,

> *Earth's fairest beauty, heaven's brightest splendor,*
> *In Jesus Christ unfolded see,*
> *All that here shineth quickly declineth*
> *Before His spotless purity.*

I have been criticized by some friends because I just can't get all excited and steamed up about earthly possessions. I just can't possibly strike an attitude of awe at a new car or anything else. I just can't. When you have seen the house or the city that hath foundations whose builder and maker is God, you can't get excited about any house in this world built by men. It was said that Abraham saw the city that had foundations whose building and maker was God and he wouldn't build a house after that. He said he would live in a tent until he received his house up there. Earth's fairest beauty and heaven's brightest splendor are all unfolded in Jesus Christ. And all that here shineth quickly declineth before His spotless purity. That's what one man said about Jesus.

I want to say it costs to know Jesus Christ like that. It costs, and most people aren't willing to pay that price. That's why most Christians are common. They won't go on because they have surrendered to evil things—things that are injurious and things that are unclean and grossly sinful. Within fundamentalism, we for the most part have given up the grossly sinful things. For Christ's sake we have surrendered those evil things. But this is the mark of a common Christian: the man who's never gone on beyond what is but a mediocre Christian.

Paul surrendered the good along with the bad. He said he not only gave up the bad things, but also things that were gain to him. Those he counted as loss. The things that he had the right to—the things that were gain to him and felt he had every legal and moral right to lay hold of and say, this is mine and Christianity is not going to take it from me—he said he had given even that up because he'd seen something so much better. It was That which was with the Father. It is that Source, that fountain from which flows all wisdom and beauty and truth and immortality. So, for the sake of That, I have given it all up. Paul knew the human heart is idolatrous and will worship anything that it possesses. Anything you get your hands on, you will worship.

We often insist upon hanging on to things. Whatever you hang on to, you worship. Possessions have the real danger of getting between you and God, whether it be property or family or reputation or security or your life itself. Jesus taught us that we can't even hang on to our own life itself. He said if we make our living on earth to be something that we won't give up and hang on to, it will get in our way and we'll lose ourselves at last. He taught that and taught it plainly.

Next is this grasping after security. We always want to be secure. Paul wasn't secure. He said he died daily. He was out on the bosom of the sea for three weeks, night and day, and he was always in difficulty. This longing for security—I want. I want security in this life and eternal security in the world above. That's fundamentalism—security here and eternal security there. Paul said I give it all out. I disavow and disown everything.

There were, though, certain things God did let him have. He let him have a book or two. He let him have a garment, a cloak. He let him have his own hired house for two years in one instance and certain other things as well. But Paul never allowed them to touch his heart. Any external treasure that touches your heart is a curse. Paul said, I give that up that I might know Him; that I might go on to a deeply enriched and increasing intimacy with vast expanses of knowledge of the One who is infinite and illimitable in His beauty. His deep desire was "that I might know

Him." Giving this all up, he never allowed anything to touch his heart.

We have been taught in Christian circles that Christ is something to add on to a happy, jolly, rather clean, but worldly and earthly life; to save us from hell and to get us into the mansions over there. But that's not the New Testament way of looking at things. It's not the way Paul looked at it. Paul saw that Jesus Christ was so infinitely attractive that he didn't count anything at all, that is, to amount to anything. Paul was a learned man. Learned at the feet of Gamaliel. He had what we would now call a PhD. He described it all as dross, even garbage—"it's no good"—and put it all behind him. He listed his accomplishments: I am of the tribe of Benjamin and circumcised the eighth day. I belong to the fathers and I've got the marks upon me and my name's inked in the register. I can show you who I am. But, he said, for the sake of Jesus Christ, I count that nothing at all. I put that all under my feet.

Let us let *The Cloud of Unknowing* talk to us again. The old writer says, "One thing I tell thee, He's a jealous lover and He suffers no rival." That's what is the matter with us. We have allowed rivals to come up. No one who has any self-respect is going to suffer a rival, but he says God won't suffer a rival. In the old English he says, "and Him list not work in thy will but He only with thee by Himself." In today's language he says that God won't work in your will unless He can only be there by Himself. We have too many gods. We have too many irons in the fire and too much theology we don't understand. We have too much religion and too much "churchianity" and too much institutionalism. The result is, God isn't in there by Himself. He says, "If I am not in your heart all by Myself, I won't work." When Jesus Christ has everything cleansed from the temple and dwells in there alone, He'll work.

Old Fénelon talked about his God's working like a miner in the depths of the earth. Have you ever been in a coal mine, way deep down in the earth where they're mining out coal or gold or diamonds? Anyone can fly or walk overhead or travel by and never dream of what's going on in the depths of the hill; never knowing that way below in that hill unseen, there's an intelligent force at work bringing out jewels. And so said Fénelon— that's what God does in the human breast. He works hidden and unseen within the breast. But we're dramatic in our day. We don't want God to work unless He comes with great fanfare. We want Him to be theatrical and do things with a good deal of color and fireworks. God doesn't work like that.

God says, no, no, no, you children of Adam, you children of carnality and lust. You who love a fair showing of flesh. You who have been brought up wrong and have wrong ideas about My Son. I won't, I won't work in you. Jesus says, I can't do it. I'm sorry. I can't work in you nor in your will or in your heart unless I can be there alone. You may need to cleanse your temple by getting busy, and throw out the cattle and upset the money changers and shovel out the dirt and get rid of a lot of things that are rivaling the Lord Jesus Christ. Remember the motto, "He's a jealous lover, and He suffereth no rival."

The Cloud of Unknowing goes on to say, "Lift up thine heart now unto God with a meek stirring of love and mean Himself and none of these goods. And as thou thereto look, loathe to think on aught but Himself, so that nothing work in thy mind nor in thy will but only Himself." I looked up the word "loathe" in the unabridged dictionary. It's an old Anglo-Saxon word meaning unwilling, be unwilling, hate. This brings us back to where we started when I said that A. B. Simpson in earlier days talked about "Himself." He shocked and blessed his generation because he talked about Himself, Jesus Himself. It's Himself that we need.

Dr. Simpson expressed it well in a message he gave at a Bible conference in London, and later created a gospel song by the same name. The story is told how he got up and took one word for each text, *Himself*. And he gave his testimony about how he had tried to get the victory. He said, "Sometimes I would get it and think I had it, and then I would lose it." Simpson went on to say, "When I came to the knowledge that victory, sanctification, deliverance, purity, holiness, all is Himself," he said after that it was easy, and the glory came to his life. He then wrote his famous hymn—

> *Once it was the blessing, now it is the Lord,*
> *Once it was the feeling, now it is His Word;*
> *Once His gift I wanted, now, the Giver own,*
> *Once I sought for healing, now Himself alone.*

There has got to be more of Himself these days. Unfortunately, Christianity has become too often a way to just get things from God. Some would give a tithe of 10 percent in order that their nine-tenths will go further than the one-tenth they gave. If a man wants to be a businessman and use God, okay, but that's not what the Bible teaches, and that's not what Paul talked about. Paul had given that up years before. That's not what the old writer of *The Cloud of Unknowing* talked about either. He said, it's only Himself. And he said, "Do this in thee is to forget all the creatures that ever God made and the works of them, so that thy thought nor thy desire be not directed nor extended to any of them, neither in general nor in special. Both let them be, and take no heed of them."

There is a danger for the Christian to get to a point where he makes Christianity to be a way to have a prosperous life down here and then secure a mansion as well in the sky. Either way, you win. If you follow the Lord, you'll prosper down here. Friend, to follow the Lord doesn't always mean to have financial prosperity. Down through the years, following the Lord has meant to count those things but loss for the excellency of the knowledge of Christ. When a person prospers in spite of himself and learns God's way, he gives everything away—as much as he can—and keeps enough to live on. Thank God, he has all the basics to sustain life, and beyond that, he's not too much concerned.

We have often seen Christianity made to be a way or technique by which we can get things. The apostle Paul knew better than that when he said, "Yea doubtless, and I count all things but loss for the excellency of the knowledge of Christ Jesus my Lord: for whom I have suffered the loss of all things, and do count them but dung, that I may win Christ, and . . . that I may know him, and the power of his resurrection" (Phil. 3:8–10). Now, it's Himself, he said. Let them be and take no heed to them.

Many would like to have a deeper spiritual life that could be given with a syringe, or something that could be given to you with a glass of water and a pill with directions to take one pill three times a day, but we know you just can't do that. That's the way some people get their religion. They want it in pill form. They buy books so they can get it in pill form. Friend, there isn't any such thing. There's a cross. There's a gallows. There's a man with stripes on His back. There is an apostle with no property. There's a tradition of loneliness and weariness and rejection and glory, but no pills as some want. But I say Himself, Himself, Himself! Personally, I don't wish for anything. I pray for it. If it isn't God's will, I don't want it. If it is God's will, I don't wish; I pray.

I would like to recapture—once more before I die—some of the glory that men knew of the beauty of Jesus. Emma Hopper once said, "Many beauteous names thou bearest" in a poem she wrote about Jesus:

> *Many beauteous names thou bearest,*
> *Brother, Shepherd, Friend, and King,*
> *But they none unto my spirit*
> *Such divine support can bring.*
>
> *Ishi, Ishi is the jewel,*
> *Mine he is while ages roll;*
> *Angels taste not of such glory,*
> *Holy Ishi of the soul.*
>
> *Other joys are short and fleeting;*
> *Thou and I can never part;*
> *Thou art altogether lovely,*
> *Ishi, Ishi of my heart.*

Ishi is Hebrew for "my husband" or "my man." They once sang that, and while I think we could sing it here, there aren't many places where you can truthfully sing it, because people don't have the experience that it conveys.

Whenever a good song such as this is rejected, it's rejected as a rule because people don't understand it and find it dull. If you only like modern music, you won't like "Ishi." And if you like something like "Tenderly He Watches over Me," you won't like "Ishi."

> *Ishi, Ishi is the jewel,*
> *Mine he is while ages roll;*
> *Angels taste not of such glory,*
> *Holy Ishi of the soul.*

This is the teaching of the deeper life. It is to put away all the creatures that God ever made and stop trying to promote your family. Stop trying to promote your business by using God to do it. Stop trying to use God to get things, and in turn, put everything away but God. "For He lists not work in thy heart unless He can be there alone." Put everything else out. We can use the Lord for anything, or try to use Him. What I am trying to say and what Paul taught here and brought down through the centuries to us today is exactly the opposite. "O God, we don't want anything you have; we want Thee." That's the cry of the soul on his way up. That's the cry of the soul.

In England, there is a bird called the skylark. We don't have them here. The nearest thing we have to it is what we call the wild canary—the American goldfinch—a poor, little, weak example of the skylark. They say the skylark will mount higher and higher and sing as it mounts. Poets have written many verses about the skylark which mounts and sings hymns at heaven's gates. As it mounts until it's out of sight, you can still hear the song coming down even though it can no longer be seen rising and singing.

My friend, if you have two knees, and even if you're stiff with arthritis and unable to get on your knees, you can look up in your heart. Prayer isn't getting on your knees. Prayer is the elevation of the heart to God. That's all a man needs. You can pray in a prison. You can pray on an airplane. You can pray anywhere and worship God, because it's Himself that we want—Himself.

> *Love sits on His eyelids and scatters delight*
> *Through all the wide regions above;*
> *Their faces the cherubim veil in His sight,*
> *And tremble with raptures of love.*
> —Joseph Swain, 1791

The only kind of revival that I'm even remotely interested in is a revival that will cause people to tremble with rapture in the presence of the Lord Jesus Christ. That's all. Do you agree?

The old writer from *The Cloud of Unknowing* says that if you're going to go on and now know God in His fullness, get up and stir yourself and lift your heart to God and put away things and desire for property and things, and seek Himself alone. Let Him work in you without any rival. In his actual words *The Cloud* author says, "All the fiends will be furious when thou doest this. And they will try to defeat thee in all that they can do." You won't even get to the corner without some fiend following after you. If you want security, don't seek God. If you want security, the devil will give it to you for a while and then send you to hell. If you're afraid of fiends and all the rest, don't try to seek God.

But he continues and says this, and I like it: "Let not, therefore, but travail therein till thou feel list." *Let not* means don't be hindered. Don't let anybody hinder you in your seeking after God, "but travail therein until you feel desire." These old saints were all such practical men. People today claim they were dreamers. They weren't dreamers. They were practical men. He said when you first start out to seek a new height and become something other than a common Christian, the first thing you'll face is the devil trying to stop you. The old saint exhorted his readers not to stop because of that, but press right on whether you feel like it or not.

There are two times to pray: when you feel like it and when you don't. The old saints knew this. They knew there are times when you've got to, by what the anonymous writer calls "a naked intent unto God." That's what we need, a naked intent to know God, to know Christ, to put the world beneath our feet, to put things beneath our feet, to put people beneath our feet, to open our hearts to only one Lover—that's the Son of God Himself—and keep everything else out of us. You can have all the relationships—husband and wife, father and son, mother and daughter, businessman and partner, taxpayer and citizen. All those, we keep outside of ourselves. But in the deep of our hearts, we have only one Lover, and He suffers no rival.

Now, why does God make us do it this way? It's to the intent that your understanding and reason get broken down and your whole case be thrown back on God. And from there on, we mount and go up. I have often said I don't think anyone has ever been filled with the Holy Spirit who didn't go through a time of awful darkness, and what the author called a cloud of unknowing, a shadowy cloud where you couldn't seem to get through. But you believed God, you trusted Christ, and whether you felt like it or not, you went on and you believed; you obeyed and you prayed when you felt like it, and you prayed when you didn't. And you obeyed and did what you should, and straightened things out and got adjusted in your business and got adjusted in your home and got adjusted in your relationships. You also quit wrong things and you gave up things that had been hindering you whether you felt like it or not. He says it's all a naked intent unto God.

Here's a strange thing: If you talk about mysticism in the day in which we live, every fundamentalist will throw his hands high in the air and say, "Why, they are dreamers. They believe in the emotion and feeling."

Every ancient writer that I'm acquainted with taught that you have got to believe God by a naked, cold intent of your will; then the other things follow along. Is it possible that we find the hard, cold, square doctrines of theology are not enough? Is it possible that people everywhere are seeking something better? Yes, it's possible, altogether possible, more than possible. But remember, "Thou feelest in thy will only a naked intent unto God."

Do you have a naked intent unto God? If so, this will bring the cross into your life. If you are going to be that kind of Christian, you're not going to let anybody stop it or fool you. You're going to keep right on, and if you don't feel like it, you're going to believe anyway. You're going to pray right on through the cold, naked intent unto God, believing the truth. And out of your stony grief, He'll raise a Bethel. Out of the tomb, He'll lift you into the sky. Out of the darkness, He'll lift you into the Life.

If you and I get Himself, we'll get all the joy and delight and all the rest with it. I'm often seen as a hard man in some ways, but there are times when the joy of the Lord lifts my heart very, very high. There are times when there is such a joy and lift toward God that I could scream out my joy. Do you want what I'm talking about? I hope so. I hope it is your desire to move on past the lower level of the common Christian and go on to know Him and the power of His resurrection and the fellowship of His suffering and the excellency of His knowledge in increasing flights of spiritual elevation.

5

SUPERIOR INTENTIONS

In our study based primarily in Philippians 3, the apostle Paul shares his personal testimony of God's work in his life. In doing so, he shares with us a number of spiritual objectives. In light of this, each serious follower of Christ should carefully consider these objectives as well. One objective is to know Christ. Another is to win Christ and to know the power of Christ's resurrection. It is to be conformed to His death. It is to experience in us that which we have in Christ. And in order to do that we must count all things as loss for the excellency of this knowledge.

In the first chapter of this book, I read the prayer of the anonymous author of *The Cloud of Unknowing*, who says he wants God to so help him that we may have the intents of our heart so cleansed that we may perfectly love God and worthily praise Him. I want to ask you, in the light of the New Testament, does it sound fanatical for us to seek a place in God where we may perfectly love Him and worthily praise Him, and be united with Him not only judicially, but experientially?

Should we not agree with both Paul and the ancient writer

that we might know Christ and win Him and know His power and conform to His death and gain a superior resurrection? Is it not also spiritually reasonable that we too should experience within ourselves that which the Scriptures clearly state we have in Christ, and be united with Him both experientially as well as judicially here in this present world? If so, why don't we relax and say this is not fanaticism, but is clearly New Testament Christianity? The Holy Spirit seems to have a twofold objective here, one of which is to convince Christians that which I am teaching is possible, and then to lead them in as Joshua led Israel into the Promised Land.

Now, the first of these is not hard—that is, to convince Christians what I am teaching is not hard but possible in this life, because there are some who are ready to accept this willingly, with the exception of a few diehards. Universities and colleges and Bible schools and conferences of every kind of evangelical and fundamentalist persuasion are asking for this. It's not hard to convince Christians these things are true, but it is impossible to lead them into it. For men it's totally impossible, but it is not impossible for the Spirit of God. For it must be the Holy Spirit that leads any of us into this place of what we call a special kind of Christian, superior to and different from the common Christian.

Over three hundred years ago, the old saint François Fénelon said, "A persuaded mind and even a well-intentioned heart is a long way from exact and faithful practice." Nothing has been more common in every age and still more so today. Nothing has been more common than to meet souls who are perfect and saintly in speculation. The Savior of the world, though, says you will know them by their works and by their behavior. "This is one rule which is never deceiving and by it we should judge ourselves," said Fénelon.

I want to give you yet another little phrase out of *The Cloud of Unknowing* which sums up the teaching of the Bible as well. It says this: "See who by grace see may." I want you to remember this. "See who by grace see may," or to put it in our modern English, let those see who can see by the grace of God. To put it in the language of the Scripture, "He that hath ears to hear, let him hear" (Matt. 11:15). He that hath eyes to see, let him see, for he talks about eyes instead of ears. See who by grace see may. God sifts out those who cannot see in order that He may lead on by grace those who can see. Remember that though Israel be as the sands of the seashore, yet a remnant shall be saved. And the Lord said in the last days few should be found who were right. The love of many should wax cold.

Let's consider the man Gideon. Gideon prepared to go up against the enemy with 32,000 soldiers. The Lord told Gideon, "You've got too many." Let them go who by grace may. So, he told everyone that was afraid to turn back, and 22,000 out of the 32,000 turned back. God said, you've still got too many. I can see people among you that cannot see, whom you'll never be able to make Israelite soldiers out of; test them. So, he took them to the river and tested them. When it was all over, he was left with three hundred soldiers. God showed He was not thinking about numbers, but about quality. God sifts out those who cannot see, but see who by grace see may. And He leads on those who by grace do see.

If your efforts to go on with God have only gotten you into

more bumps, remember Christ's journey to immortal triumph. Remember the garden where He sweat blood. Remember Pilate's hall where they put a purple robe on Him and smote Him. Remember the desertion when they all forsook Him and fled. Remember the journey up the hill to Calvary. Remember the nailing on the cross. Remember the six hours. Remember the hiding of the Father's face. Remember the darkness, and remember the surrender of His spirit in death. This was the path that Jesus took to immortal triumph and everlasting glory. And as He is, so are we in this world.

This is what some call the dark night of the soul. Scarcely is a Christian willing to go into this dark night of the soul. That is why there are very few Christians that ever enter into the light. They don't know the morning because they won't know the night. I have had people come to me and say, "Mr. Tozer, I have known quite a while this darkness of which you speak. God has chopped me down and cut me down and He's knocked down my business and I've actually been tempted by the devil, but the morning hasn't come in my heart. Why does it take so long?" Here's what the author of *The Cloud of Unknowing* says: "This work asketh no long time before it be once truly done as some men wean," that is to say, some men think or believe. "For it is the shortest work of all that men may imagine. It is neither longer nor shorter, but even according to the stirring that is within thee, even thy will." The stirrings within thee aren't enough. There isn't a vacuum in there yet.

And so, the Holy Spirit can't rush in because there's not enough stirring within. The reality is, everybody is as full as he wants to be. And everybody is as holy as he wants to be. And when we think we want and don't, then of course we wonder why it takes so long. I'll tell you why we haven't gone on faster and why those who are seeking have not come up into the land yet. It is because they have not come to the end of themselves. We often interfere with God's working in us. He wills thou but look on Him and let Him alone, but God can't get us to let Him alone. We struggle to keep up a good front instead of being humble and meek. Christians want a good front. There's hardly a Christian that doesn't want to go to heaven when he dies to see old Jordan roll, but he wants to have a good front while he's here. It is a clear teaching of the Bible that we ought to expose our inner state to God, but we often attempt to hide our inner state. And because we hide our inner state, God can't change that inner state. We hide it and disguise our poverty of spirit.

If we were suddenly to look on the outside the way we do within our souls to Almighty God, we would be the most embarrassed people of all. There would be people barely able to stand. There would be people in rags. There would be people completely too dirty to be decent. There would be people that have great sores on their bodies. There would be persons that even Skid Row would turn out. But we won't let God know how poor we are in spirit, and we won't tell it. That is why we have to wait so long. And that is why we want to go on with God, but we don't. We disguise our poverty of spirit and hide our inward state to preserve our reputation.

And then we want to keep some authority to ourselves. We don't want to turn the last key over to Jesus Christ. We want to have dual controls and let the Lord run it, but have controls before us in case the Lord fails. So, we're not turning over all the authority. We just don't intend to, and that's why we have to wait so long. We want to keep some glory for ourselves. We want a little bit. We're willing to sing the glory be Thine and Thine is the kingdom and the glory, but we want a little glory for ourselves.

Fénelon also said this: "We are strangely ingenious in perpetually seeking our own interests. What worldly souls do crudely and openly, people who want to live for God often do more subtly." Do you get that? It's almost humorous. But it is so true that we're strangely ingenious with an ability to seek our own interests under the guise of seeking the interests of God. Because of this truth, I have no difficulty in stating there are thousands of people who are using missions and healing and prophecy and the deeper life and all the rest for no other purpose than to secretly promote their own private interests. They are using it as a pretext and letting the pretext serve them as a screen so they'll never know how really ugly they are on the inside.

Now, we contradict, I say, because we seek to rescue ourselves from the cross. Nobody wants to die on a cross, and yet Paul said, I want to die on that cross, and I want to know what it is to die on the cross. And in order that if I die like Him, I might have a superior resurrection. Those who know the Greek know that's what He said. He didn't say "so He'll raise me from the dead." Every Christian will be raised from the dead, but he said, I want a resurrection like His, a superior resurrection. And in order to do it, I've got to die like Him. We're willing to die a little bit, and we're willing to die a piece at a time, but we're always wanting to rescue a little part of ourselves from the cross, and it's that part of yourselves that you rescue that keeps you in trouble all the time.

It's entirely possible to contradict ourselves. It's entirely possible to beg to be filled and yet resist the filling; beg and plead to be filled and yet hinder God from filling us. He wishes and wills thou do but look on Him and let Him alone. And so, we beg to be filled and seem to resist the filling, and there's that strange ingenuity. There's that strange contradiction within us that our wills won't stir enough. And what worldly people do crudely, we who live for God often do more subtly. Before God, of course, it isn't subtle, but it is before us. Thus, we contradict ourselves and that's the problem. We live in a state of contradiction. We beg, "Fill me now." We resist God and say, "Fill me now."

There's a part of us we won't let die. We want to keep it alive. And we're never going to let anybody know the poverty of our spirit or the terrible condition of our inward state. We're going to preserve our reputation and our glory, a little glory, and thus live in a state of perpetual contradiction. That's one reason why Christians are not happy. A man who is always on a cross isn't happy. It's when he gets over with that and says, "Into Thy hand I commend my spirit" and ceases to defend himself, and lets go, it's then that he dies. But also, there's a resurrection that follows.

If we are ever going to be anything other than common, mediocre Christians—Christians halfway up from where we ought to be, halfway up the peak, not to heaven, but halfway up to where we ought to be (that's what mediocre means)—we will never grow in Christ until we have given up our own interests and put ourselves in God's hands, and let God alone. We want to tell God what He ought to do.

We read the life of Adoniram Judson and we say, "Now God, I want You to do that." Or we read about D. L. Moody's life and then we say, "Lord, we want You to do what You did for Moody." Now, God could pour the Holy Spirit on you walking down the street in Philadelphia, but we want to tell God how to do it and at the same time preserve a little bit of the glory and keep some areas in our lives that have not been crucified. We want to be crucified technically, but nobody wants it in reality. Until we put ourselves in the hand of God and let Him alone, we'll just be what we are: mediocre Christians singing happy songs to keep from being completely blue, trying to keep up a little the best we can. If we are not making progress and don't know what it is to be one with Him experientially and have the intents of our hearts so cleansed, it will be impossible to perpetually love Him and worthily praise Him.

There are some whose knuckles are white from hanging on to the windowsill, and the Lord's been saying to you, "Look unto Me and let go." But you won't do it. You just won't do it. You are not going to do it. You're going to go to heaven. You couldn't miss that because you've accepted Christ. We know that by the books, but Paul says,

That I may know him, and the power of his resurrection, and the fellowship of his sufferings, being made conformable unto his death. . . . Brethren, I count not myself to have apprehended: but this one thing I do, forgetting those things which are behind, and reaching forth unto those things which are before [and you're afraid to], I press toward the mark for the prize of the high calling of God in Christ Jesus. (Phil. 3:10, 13–14)

"See who by grace see may" and the rest can sit around, get old, and wait for the undertaker. Go to conferences year after year and get nothing out of them. Hear sermons year after year and not get anything. Go to Bible studies year after year and not make any progress, and just barely keep your chin up above the water. See who by grace see may. But we're ingenious, surprisingly ingenious in fixing our Christian life so we get a little glory out of it and get our own way, instead of entering God's way.

In my Christian and Missionary Alliance fellowship, we're supposed to be a deeper life church in which we believe there's a life of supreme victory in Christ, a union with Him that will lift us above our troubles and will take us through the dark valley of the dying and bring us out without the weight and burden of things; having given up everything and yet having everything; having let go, and still being safe.

Do you remember what was said about Jesus?

Let this mind be in you, which was also in Christ Jesus: who, being in the form of God, thought it not robbery to be equal with God: but made himself of no reputation, and took upon him the form of a servant, and was made in the likeness of men: and being found in fashion as a man, he humbled himself, and became obedient unto death, even the death of the cross." (Phil. 2:5–8)

Now, do we stop there and close the book? No.

Wherefore God also hath highly exalted him, and given him a name which is above every name: that at the name of Jesus every knee should bow, of things in heaven, and things in earth, and things under the earth; and that every tongue should confess that Jesus Christ is Lord, to the glory of God the Father." (Phil. 2:9–11)

Up out of His stony grief, He raised a Bethel. Up out of His dying came a living and an exaltation and triumphant victory.

And so it is for every child of God. We'll never conquer until He's conquered us. The way we conquer our enemies is to let God conquer us. Don't rush out at your enemy; just submit and let God conquer you. And by doing that, God has conquered every enemy. Will you do it? Are you interested? Would you like to be supremely victorious in this life, filled with God's Spirit, gifted of His Spirit to walk out as a special kind of Christian; not to be proud of it, but to be uniquely and meekly, humbly thankful? By the good grace of God, you see who by grace see may. That is, he that hath ears to hear, let him hear.

6

OUR ACTIVE WILL

T hen said I, Lo, I come: in the volume of the book it is written of me, I delight to do thy will, O my God: yea, thy law
is within my heart" (Ps. 40:7–8).

Reduced to its simplest terms, all spiritual perfection, or maturity, is no more and no less than to do the will of God. I would
like to address the will of God and its relation to our cross.

Hell is the place where the will of God is never done, and that
is why it is hell. Heaven is the place where it is always done, and
that is why it is heaven. But between hell and heaven there is the
earth. Earth is the place where the will of God is either not done
at all, as in the unsaved world, or only partly done, as among
most of us Christians, or imperfectly done.

Our relation to the will of God is twofold: passive and active.
It is passive in that it is in resignation to God's acts. We sing
about the will of God, and when we do, we usually mean what
Mary meant when she said, "Be it unto me according to thy
word" (Luke 1:38). That was something God was going to do
but not something that she was doing. That is resignation in pas-

sivity. That is saying, "God, I accept Thy will for me. Go ahead, and whatever You send is all right with me;" and that is necessary and good.

There is also a second relation to the will of God, and that is the active side of the will of God—voluntary observance of God's commandments. That is to make such changes as God indicates, to drop some things and take up others, and to bring the entire life into accord with the New Testament. That is what I call reformation in the church, and if pursued, it would result in a revival. But if it cannot come yet to the whole church, then it can come to as many as will receive it through the active, voluntary observance of God's commandments.

I once heard a great sermon by Paul Rader in which he preached that God heard Elijah because Elijah heard God. He pointed out that God did according to the word of Elijah because Elijah had done according to the Word of God. You can't separate these two things. There's a great lot of passive sitting about singing "Have Thine own way, Lord, have Thine own way"—and we don't know what it's going to be. We're passively resigned. But that is only a part of it. The other part is to hear the voice of God and do what we're told, and that means active. That means bringing the entire life into accord with the New Testament's teaching—Bible teaching.

The will of God, I will say to you, is the place of blessed, painful, fruitful trouble. Paul called it the fellowship of His sufferings. It is my conviction that one of the reasons we have so little of post-cross power is because we will not have pre-cross trouble. And because we will not let the will of God trouble us, we want to be passive. But we will not allow the will of God to trouble us.

Paul called it the fellowship of His sufferings. Don't forget, at the fellowship of His sufferings you will find Christ in clear manifestation. If there's anything in this world I want, it is to have a clear and continuous manifestation of that Presence, that One in whose presence my soul takes delight. We do not have it because we do not relate the will of God to the cross.

The great saints were acquainted with the cross even before Christ's time. And before that cross was raised on the bloody hill, they were acquainted with it in essence because their obedience brought it to them. There was Jacob, whose cross came from his own carnal self. It is my belief that Christians ought to be exorcised in spirit very frequently. They ought to be in trouble with their own hearts frequently, and if they are not, it is probably because they do not know their own heart. Jacob didn't at first, but did later and knew his own heart. Jacob's cross was Jacob, the worst possible kind of cross a man can deal with. It was Jacob himself. And then there was Daniel, whose cross was the world. Job's cross was the devil. So, we have the world, the flesh, and the devil in Jacob, Daniel, and Job. The devil crucified Job, and the world crucified Daniel. Jacob was crucified on the tree of his own Jacob-ness—his own carnality.

Looking at Moses we find his cross was the oppressor of God's people. And there were the apostles. Their cross came from the religious authorities. And there was Luther. His cross came from the church that makes so much of wooden crosses, the Catholic Church. And there was Wesley, and his cross came from the Protestant church. And I could go on down the line and name many great souls who had crosses in the will of God and who followed the will of God to their cross. In many cases it was before Christ's time and after His death on that cross when Paul said afterwards, "I am crucified with Christ" (Gal. 2:20). By faith, they all looked forward and discovered their obedience to the will of God led them into the place of blessed and painful and fruitful trouble.

When we talk about our cross, it is important to state that we cannot go up on the hillside and die. Following Jesus physically when He was on earth was the easiest, cheapest way to get out of work and say goodbye to family by just saying, "I'm going to follow Jesus." Multitudes did. They followed Him physically, but they didn't understand Him spiritually. So, the cheapest, easiest way to dispose of the cross is to carry the cross physically. That would be the easiest way to do it. But your cross isn't going to be going out and following Jesus along a dusty pathway. And it isn't going to be climbing the hill with two others and being nailed up between them. Our cross will be the trouble we get our own hearts into by obedience to the will of God. In this is our identification.

Our Plymouth Brethren friends rightly make a great deal of identification, and they should. That identification, that oneness with Christ or, as Paul said, oneness in crucifixion, brings us into oneness in spirit. This rang true with the anonymous writer of *The Cloud of Unknowing*, in which he taught that men should seek to be *oned* with God. It is the purpose of this study that some earnest Christians might take this effort seriously and seek to be *oned* with God in a way many in the evangelical world consider fanaticism.

Resurrection is another word. There are some men who preach death so much they never get anyone up out of death. They preach death, death, death. When I was a young fellow, I was wonderfully filled with the Holy Spirit and was getting along quite well; that is, until I read a book about the cross. That particular book put me on the cross in the first chapter, and as far as I can remember, I was still hanging on the cross in the last chapter. The result was, it was gloomy all the way through. The author himself wasn't a gloomy man, but somehow he got that gloom into his book and I had an awful time shaking it off. It took me a long time to get away from the gloominess of it.

There was a preacher back beyond that time by the name of A. B. Simpson whose approach to this cross was so radiantly wonderful that he jarred and blessed a generation. He taught that there is a cross. But beyond the cross, there's a resurrection and an identification and a manifestation. Do you know, the most desirable thing that would bring tears of joy to your eyes every time you thought of it would be if you could have a loving nearness of the Savior bestowed upon you and were to experience a sudden bestowal of a Presence. That has always been the way He comes. I want to see that.

I would consider it the greatest favor He's done for me yet that there should be a sudden manifestation. I don't mean rolling in the aisles. I don't mean yelling. I don't mean tongues. I don't mean any physical manifestation at all, except that it would result in that tenderest manifestation of tears of joy. I just mean a Presence made known to the spirit. That's all. And He's willing to give that. That's what they had in the Welsh revival to such a degree that sometimes the preacher couldn't even preach. We don't see that much today, and besides, nobody wants it. That's why I say we must have reformation. We must have this back on us again before we can hope for revival that is really revival.

Now, those three words—*identification, resurrection,* and *manifestation*—they're all through the cross of our Lord Jesus Christ. I want to give you a few little sentences about the cross which I have taken from a man whose saintliness was known around the whole world and still is down to this day through *The Cloud of Unknowing.* He says, "God is ingenious in making us crosses." Think of it! God is ingenious. If we just say I am crucified with Christ by faith, that's no cross at all. That's technical. But God wants to really crucify you, so He is ingenious in making us crosses. He makes them of iron and of lead, which are heavy in themselves. And He makes them of straw, which seems to weigh nothing, yet they're no less difficult to carry. Some of these straw crosses, which to some don't seem to amount to anything, are in reality crucifying you through and through.

It often pleases God to join physical weakness to this servitude of the Spirit. The ancient writer goes on to say nothing is more useful than these two crosses together. They crucify a man from head to foot. Did you know Jesus Christ was crucified from head to foot? Did you know that when they nailed Him to the cross, He was crucified all over? There wasn't a part of His holy nature that was not pained by the cross. He was crucified from head to foot. God takes pleasure in thus confounding human power, which is only weakness disguised.

Whatever kind of intellectual power you have, such as a great mind, it will bother you and get you in trouble, but it's a good thing to have if God has so ordered. It is just weakness disguised. Do you have talents? They are just weakness disguised, and everything you have is just human weakness disguised. God takes great pleasure in confounding it.

The Cloud of Unknowing author says God wants to make what the world most admires ridiculous and frightful, so He treats without pity those whom He raises without measure. And He joins these crosses and crucifies the man from head to foot because He wants to raise him without measure. I quote once again from what the apostle Paul said in Philippians 2:5–8:

> Let this mind be in you, which was also in Christ Jesus: who, being in the form of God, thought it not robbery to be equal with God: but made himself of no reputation, and took upon him the form of a servant, and was made in the likeness of men: and being found in fashion as a man, he humbled himself, and became obedient unto death, even the death of the cross.

Do you know the next words? "Wherefore God also hath highly exalted him, and given him a name which is above every name: that at the name of Jesus every knee should bow . . . and that every tongue should confess" (Phil. 2:9–11).

God will crucify without pity those whom He wants to raise without measure. I believe this. And then *The Cloud of Unknowing* adds this rather beautiful and almost half-humorous expression. He says, "How beautiful it is to have our purgatory where others seek to have their paradise." How wonderful it is to get your purgatory where other people are looking for their paradise. Everyone else wants their paradise down below, and this wise old brother says you can have your purgatory here. You won't have to wait to go to a nonexistent purgatory after death, but right down here where others are seeking their fun and their best, with their entertainments and amusements and all the rest. If you're walking with God and you're letting the will of God lead you into that place, that cross, that place of blessed, fruitful trouble—your own heart—how beautiful that you can have your purgatory here.

And *The Cloud of Unknowing* continues by saying, "Suffering then is only a matter of being silent before God, for it is God who brings to birth within us dryness." It is God who brings to birth within you dryness and impatience and discouragement to humiliate you and to show you yourself. It is He who does it all. We have only to see Him and adore Him, to adore Him while He slays us and to love Him while He crucifies us. For He says He crucifies without pity those He raises without measure.

Oh, do you want to be raised without measure? Do you want God to say to all the angels and all the creatures that do His will, "The lid's off for this man"? "There's no limit to where I'll take him. There's no measure, no ceiling on what he can have. Just keep it open. There's no top to it. Without measure I'll raise him. And it's because without pity, I'll crucify him." What does he mean? He says, "Happy are they who in this state consider the hand of God which crucifies them through pity." He crucifies without pity, and He crucifies through pity.

You that have had the care of children, you know what it is to punish without pity and yet punish with pity. Do you know what it is when you pray for your child and you want that child to be the very finest example of a good citizen? You love them until you would give your blood out of your veins for them. And yet without pity, you spare not the rod. And yet what is it? It is pity that makes you punish them without pity. Do you see the beautiful mix-up there? That's the way God feels. It is the pity of God over His children. Let Him spare not the rod that He might make us the kind of people He wants us to be.

It is God who does it all. And we have only to see Him and to adore Him in it all. There will be a time, not far distant, when all you will have will be God and the cross. It is that cross which is yours by being in the will of God. It may come from any direction. Mine usually comes from within when God lets me fall on my face or break a nose or do some fool thing or otherwise injure my soul. That's the cross, and the Lord nails me there. All we have to do is see Him and adore Him in it all. Looking forward only to identification, manifestation, resurrection, and power, can you say, "O God, crucify me from head to foot—from head to foot, God"?

This is the reformation we need now. Once they needed a reformation that would bring the Bible back to the church. They got it. When they needed a reformation that would teach men to trust Christ Jesus and be justified and cleansed, they got it under the Wesleys. We now need a reformation that shall take the will of God and adore it, and look on God and let Him work, looking not backward, but looking forward. We need to disassociate from everything, however sound it may seem in doctrine, but all that which is unspiritual and all that is un-Christlike and all that isn't New Testament, and look on Him and let Him work and say, "O cross! O good cross! I embrace thee."

Did you ever stop to think that Easter came after Good Friday? There had to be Good Friday before there could be Easter. Before He could rise and sing among His brethren, He had to bow His head and suffer among His brethren. And this is what is lost from the church. The only suffering we know about is that which is imposed by accident from the outside. And then we write books about it and make heroes of people that wouldn't have had it that way if they could have gotten out of it. They have no credit coming because it happened to them by accident. That's no cross. Your cross is what you take from the hand of God, looking on Him and letting Him work and thanking Him and adoring Him. And you wouldn't change it if you could, and you could but you won't.

Then comes the glorious resurrection. Then comes the life and the blessing. Before there can come the radiance of the dawn, there must be the darkness of the night. Before there can come the life of resurrection, there must be the death that ends another kind of life. "O cross! O good cross! . . . I adore in thee the dying Jesus."

Here's a little prayer I wrote a long time ago: "O God, let me die right rather than live wrong." Rather than live a poor life down on a low level, I'd rather reach a high spot and turn off the light. I would rather die right than live wrong. O blessed cross of Jesus. O will of God Supreme. O sweet will of God. Do you know anything about it? Are you in it? Has it done anything for you or to you? Have you known the place of sweet, blessed trouble and of heart-searching and of travail? If you haven't, you can never know the blessing and the glory. You can pray for revival until you die and you'll never experience revival. You can join groups and pray all night for revival, and all you will lose is sleep, and all you'll gain will be exercise.

If we believe in this kind of reformation, that costs what may, why not do something about it? Why don't we come to the Lord and say, "O blessed will of God, blessed will of God, O blessed cross, for I adore my blessed Savior. Crucify me from head to foot"? I believe that out of your stony grief, there will be a Bethel raised.

> O Cross, that liftest up my head,
> I dare not ask to fly from Thee;
> I lay in dust life's glory dead,
> And from the ground there blossoms red,
> Life that shall endless be.

Will you come to God and lay your glory in the dust the best you know how; to come and lay your glory in the dust, and before the Lord seek the will of God for yourself in obedience; the will and the cross and the identification and the presence and the glory and the resurrection and the Life? Will you do it?

7

FINDING HIM—ALONE

Every electrician knows there are two poles in an electrical system: the positive and the negative. With that in mind, there is a vast difference in tone between our main text of study in Philippians 3, the great Bible giants, and the shining souls that have all lived since Bible times when compared with present-day gospel Christians.

Take, for instance, the man David, who sought after the Lord back in the book of Psalms: "As the hart panteth after the water brooks, so panteth my soul after thee, O God. My soul thirsteth for God, for the living God: when shall I come and appear before God?" (Ps. 42:1–2). And, "O God, thou art my God; early will I seek thee: my soul thirsteth for thee, my flesh longeth for thee in a dry and thirsty land, where no water is; to see thy power and thy glory, so as I have seen thee in the sanctuary" (Ps. 63:1–2). And then he continues and says, "My soul followeth hard after thee: thy right hand upholdeth me" (Ps. 63:8). That's the language of the man David.

You will find this type of language throughout the Old

Testament, beginning with Abraham and tracing all the way down through the ancient text. They were a thirsty lot. And the difference between them and us, and between the tone of their lives and the tone of our lives, is that they sought Him and found Him and sought Him still and found Him and sought Him again and found Him and sought Him more. But we believe on Him, accept Him, and seek Him no more. Now, there's the difference.

When I think about some great souls whose very names are music to us, it is important to understand they got their virtue from the same place we get ours—from Jesus Christ our Lord. Their merit comes from the same fountain as ours. Their names are music because they're associated with this thirst that Paul expressed here when he said he counted all things but loss. I follow after, if that I may apprehend, and I forget the things which are behind and I reach forth unto those things. It was this that gives music to the names of Augustine and Tauler and Jacob Boehme and Thomas à Kempis and Richard Rolle, and Bernard of Clairvaux and Bernard of Cluny and John of the Cross and Madame Guyon.

Why do they bring us up like tuning an instrument when we hear their names? Not that they had anything that you and I don't potentially have and by nature possess, but they were associated with the longing, thirsting crowd as did Nicholas of Cusa and John van Ruysbroeck, Lorenzo Scupoli and François Fénelon—and men who rose like Henry Suso and Samuel Rutherford. Incidentally, it was Henry Suso's brother who said there is a difference between hearing a lute sweetly played and only hearing that one has been played. And he went on to say most Christians are to this effect: they only hear there has been a lute played, but they themselves have never heard it played. Then there was Samuel Rutherford and Cooper and Heber and Samuel Swain and William Law and John Newton and Samuel Medley and Tersteegen, and Paul Gerhardt and Stennett and Doddridge.

These are musical names because we associate them with thirsty souls. We see them as the deer that's been chased by the hounds, thirsting, longing for the water, and saying, "Let me alone for my soul is seeking God"; and they found Him. What a tragedy it has been in our time that we are taught to believe on Him, accept Him, and then seek Him no more. And that's where we are today. My goal is to stir people to want to seek God. It's the heart that's crying after the One he loves, more than the heart that has settled down to what he has.

I want to point you to the Old Testament book of the Song of Solomon. Most people don't read it because they don't understand what it means. It was, though, the very joy of these great souls that I've been telling you about. Bernard started to write a series of sermons on the Song of Solomon and had only preached the sermons on the first chapter when he died. He finished it over there in glory. The Song of Solomon is a story of a girl who is very deeply in love with a young shepherd, but who is so beautiful that a king demands her favors. Despite this, she stays loyal to her simple shepherd, who gathers lilies in the dew of the night and comes to seek her and call to her through the lattice. It's quite a wonderful love story indeed. It has been understood by the church that Jesus is the shepherd, the rejected shepherd, and the world with all it offers is the king, demanding or coaxing and winning, trying to woo and win our love.

Many songs such as the following have come from this book:

> *Sweet is the odour of Thy grace.*
> *Thy name pour'd forth fills all the place*
> *   with heavenly fragrancy.*
> *Thy precious name the virgin's love,*
> *Drawn by that unction from above,*
> *They run, they cleave to Thee.*

And another:

> *Thou shepherd of Israel, and mine,*
> *   The joy and desire of my heart.*
> *For closer communion I pine—*
> *   I long to reside where Thou art.*
>
> *Ah, show me that happiest place,*
> *   That place of Thy people's abode,*
> *Where saints in an ecstasy gaze*
> *   And hang on a crucified God.*
>
> *'Tis there with the lambs of Thy flock,*
> *   There only I covet to rest,*
> *To lie at the foot of the rock,*
> *   Or rise to be hid in Thy breast.*

'Tis there I would always abide,
And never a moment depart,
Concealed in the cleft of Thy side,
Eternally held in Thine heart.

In these great songs we hear the way they talked about God. My real fear is that our flippant type of "Only Believe" Christianity today will turn our present-day evangelicalism into liberalism. Always remember that the church never runs on its head. The church runs on its heart. Always remember, the Holy Spirit never fills a man's head, but fills a man's heart. The effort today to equate Christianity with all learning and all philosophy and all science is going to get a cold frown from Almighty God. He will let them go their blind way to liberalism at last. You will see it little by little by little, protesting they're not while they are. Somewhere, God will have Himself a people. I don't know where they are, but God will have Himself a people, and they will be those who ever more cry after Him, the One they love.

I believe it is important to point out there is no place for human effort. Looking back at *The Cloud of Unknowing*, the old writer says, "Be wary in this work, travail not in thy wits nor in thy imagination." He's saying, remember in your longing after God, don't try to think your way through. In all this there is an element of unknowing, a deep, divine abyss of the Godhead— the soundless, undulating sea of Being we call God. It is there, and it's beyond the power of thought or visualization; it's utterly and completely futile in trying to think your way through. Through grace, man can have fullness of knowledge, but of God Himself can no man think. That doesn't mean that you can't think about Him, but you can't think around Him and think equal to Him and up to Him. *The Cloud* goes on to say, "He may well be loved, but not thought. By love may he be gotten but by thought never." How then can we know Him with a devout and pleasing stirring of love, to pierce that cloud of darkness and smite upon it with a sharp dart of longing love? "For it sufficeth enough, naked intent direct unto God without any other cause than Himself."

There's that word *Himself* again. I have been noticing how often that word Himself occurs. Did you know that my society, the Christian and Missionary Alliance, almost began on the word Himself—Christ Himself? And it was Himself that gave us the message. Unfortunately, we're far away from it today, being simply satisfied with the works of God and the theology of God. But you'll get there, because thought engages the intellectual element in the gospel. Remember that one of the attributes of deity is intellect, and there is an intellectual element in the gospel. That's what we call theology or doctrine. And thought engages theology. Thought engages doctrine and is necessary and right.' However, it is that which is beyond the intellect which we need and seek. It is that which you can't get to with your head.

One song says the Spirit breathes upon the Word and brings the truth to sight. When the Spirit breathes on the Scriptures, how much more wonderful the Scriptures are than when they are merely taught. When we merely hear the expounding of the Word of God without the Spirit breathing upon it, it can be a harmful, if not a useless, thing.

We sing sometimes beyond the sacred page, not apart from the sacred page, not away from the sacred page, not contrary to the sacred page, but beyond the sacred page. The sacred page is not to be a barrier to block our way to God. The sacred page is not to be a substitute for God, though it is made that by millions of people. The sacred page is not to be the end, but only the means toward the end—and God is the end. It is God we seek with a naked intent unto God. "It sufficeth enough, in naked intent directed unto God and without any other cause than Himself."

Unfortunately, the current trend is that if we have the text, we have the experience, and most evangelicals settle for that. If we have the text, we have the experience. Friend, it's all wrong. If we have the text, we simply have the text. But the experience ought to result from the text. In other words, you can have the text and not have the experience.

Many will say, am I not accepted in the beloved? Do not I have everything there is in Jesus? Is not God my Father, and am I not an heir with God? And we limp our ragged, lonely way down the street forgetting that it's one thing to have the will, and it's another thing to have what we're willed. The will of God is one thing, but to have the will of God is another thing. I want to say to you, as *The Cloud* said, "Be thou aware, and don't try to think your way through." Some have come up to a point where they have fought their way up as far as they can get and will never get any further with their head. They might just as well put it to rest.

Friend, when you meet God finally, it has to be alone in your heart. For there's a loneness, a real loneness there. People don't want to be alone. Young people for the most part don't want to be alone with God. They want the crowd around them. They want people there that can laugh. They want people there that can take the heat off. They want friends around that can give support and comfort. But if you ever get through to where you should, to the place where your longing heart finds the water, it's going to be alone. I don't mean there won't be others with you. God has to cut every maverick out of the herd and brand him all alone, all alone. He doesn't do it by mass, but it's all alone. When the Holy Spirit came at Pentecost and sat upon the three thousand, He came on each of them, said the Scripture, each of them. It didn't say it sat upon all of them en masse. The Spirit sat upon each of them. And each one went through this experience as if he had been all by himself.

God wants us to press through where there is no natural light to help us. We can't lean on anything natural. You have to find God as the roe found the water brook. You have to seek God alone. I would love to help you and quote Scripture and sing to you and do my best, but when He meets you, it will be by yourself. What we want to do is to evermore cry after Him, "Thou lovest," and look for His direction with nothing but a naked intent unto Himself, a naked intent unto God. I want God and want nothing more.

Now, what shall we do? Well, Christ has removed all the legal hindrances. For that I am glad. Jesus Christ has removed all the legal hindrances. But I believe there are legal reasons why I ought not go to heaven. I believe there are governmental reasons why I should not go to heaven. I believe that a holy God must run His universe according to holy laws, and if He runs His kingdom according to holy laws, I don't belong there because I've broken every one of them either in intent or in purpose. And so, there's got to be a justification somewhere. There's got to be a redemption somewhere. Something has to be done to legally permit me to have God and for God to have me—and it's been done. Thank God it's been done.

So remember that every illegal hindrance has been taken away. And there isn't a thing that can stop you except yourself, not a thing in the wide world. All the depths of the fullness of God are yours. And there's not a reason why we can't enter in if we still forevermore cry after Him and look unto Him with a naked intent of love.

I have pointed out to you that the only way to get in is to believe our way in. I have tried to deal with people who try to think their way in. There's a time when all you can do is believe God and believe what He says—believe and love. Believe and love. *The Cloud of Unknowing* says, "But of God Himself no man can think . . . He may well be loved, but not thought. By love may He be gotten and holden; but by thought never."

The great God Almighty that fills the universe and overflows into immensity can never be surrounded by that little thing you call your head, your intellect. Never, never, never. He knows that all you could do would be to stand at the lowest point of the shoe sole of God and think down there. You could never rise to the face of God. But love and faith rise. By these we can know God, by love and faith.

It is a very pleasant thought to know there are no vacuums in the kingdom of God. A vacuum is an empty place where there isn't anything, not even air. Nature abhors a vacuum, I am told. And wherever there's a vacuum, unless it's protected by a hard shell, air rushes in and fills it. The kingdom of God abhors a vacuum. When you empty yourself, God Almighty rushes in.

The sad reality is, we as evangelicals find ourselves where we are and simply satisfied with what we have. But if you have been actively emptying yourself, you will discover God Himself will rush into the vacuum.

The Wesley brothers once wrote, "Drawn by my Redeemer's love; after Him I follow fast, drawn from earth to things above, drawn out of myself at last." Drawn out of myself at last. Did you know that's your trouble, and with so many of us? We've never been "drawn from earth to things above, drawn out of myself at last." What a happy hour when we've been drawn out of ourselves, and there is a vacuum, and into that vacuum rushes the blessed Presence. You must know this does not consist in anything else but in the knowledge of the goodness and greatness of God; and of our own nothingness and inclination to every evil, in subjecting not only unto Him, but for love of Him unto every creature in the renunciation of all will of our own and a complete resignation of ourselves to His good pleasure. All this should be willed and done by us simply for the glory of God and for His pleasure alone, as *The Cloud* says, "because He thus wills and merits to be thus loved and served." And this is the law of God impressed by the hand of the Lord Himself in the hearts of His faithful servants.

This is His easy yoke, and this is His burden light, so wrote Scupoli, one of the great saints of other days. Here's the wonderful thing, friend. Whenever the Holy Spirit talks, He always says the same thing to everybody. I have mentioned names from Augustine or from David on down to later times. You can read their hymns and read their devotional books, and you will find that they all add up to the same thing: a Faber and a Hebert, a

Calvinist and an Armenian and an Episcopalian and a Catholic. If they lived in the day when there was power and light, they added up to the same thing—and the Holy Spirit doesn't say two things. He says one thing—He says the same thing to everybody that's listening to Him. And so, I can quote from almost anywhere and not be contradicted because the same Holy Spirit says the same thing to all of His children. He says, pour yourself out. Give yourself up to Me. Empty yourself. Bring your empty earthen vessels, not a few. Bring them and empty yourself.

It's the same thing—for the glory of God alone—that they all speak. In 1 Corinthians 1 and 2, Paul says "for God Himself," not mentality, not intellect, but the Holy Spirit. Who knoweth the things of a man, but the Spirit of the man that's in him? Who knoweth the things of God, but the Holy Spirit? You can't climb your way up Jacob's ladder hand-over-heels into the kingdom; and you can't think your way through. You can only love your way in and believe your way in and come in meekness like a child. And then, drawn by your Redeemer's love, come and pour yourself out until at last you're delivered from yourself.

You know, that's your only problem—yourself. You say, "If I had a better pastor, I'd be a better Christian." I wish that could be so, but you know, it wouldn't be. The better the pastor you could have and the better preacher he would be, the more peril you'd be in, because you would tend to become a spiritual parasite and lean on him. Often the most spiritual people are in churches where their pastor can't preach his way out of a wet paper sack. The reason they are deeply spiritual is because they have no help from the pulpit, so they seek God alone. I believe in the priesthood of believers. And I believe there are men who hear the voice of God as surely as I do and have as much right to speak as I have.

So, my friend, it's just you that are your troubles. It's just you, and if you will get delivered from yourself, drawn out of yourself at last, what a noise it will be when you're drawn out of yourself. When you are stuck so far down in the mud of your own ego that when God pulls you out, there will be a sound that can be heard a block away. And paraphrasing *The Cloud*, "God can be loved and by a love He may be gotten and by a love He may be holden, but by thought never."

So we should be careful. Don't try to enter into a deeper spiritual life by your wits or your imagination. Don't try it, but look unto God by yourself. Seek God in your own heart. It is not wrong to go to altars and prayer rooms and pray. I'm talking about the loneliness of the soul that may be cut out of the crowd, cut out all by himself even as a little woman pushed herself toward Jesus as He was so crushed in the crowd as they were pressing Him on every side. One lonely, little woman surrounded and pushed and jostled and touched His hem and was healed. He turned and said, "Who touched me?" He could have said, "Who touched me in faith? Who touched me with love?" The rest of the crowd that day were merely jostled. We have meetings where people just jostle the Lord. That's all, just jostle Him. He's there, but they're just jostling.

Somewhere, some little soul will push through and touch Him, and in love and in faith, he or she will touch Him and their heart will be healed. Do you know what many of us need? We need to have our hearts healed. We need to have the ointment put on our hearts. Is there no balm in Gilead? Yes, yes, yes. There is a balm in Gilead to heal the sin-sick soul. I don't know what else I can say other than to say to you, your Beloved is gathering lilies, and if you watch, you'll see Him put His hand through the lattice and say, come, My beloved. Rise up where the rain is over and gone and the singing of the birds is heard in the land.

Oh, my friend, He's very near to us, and He'll never be anyplace but very near. He's grieved and He's sad. But He's very near and He waits. He waits for a vacuum to form inside your heart. You say, what is in my heart? Well, I don't know, but whatever it is, it's got to get out. And when you pour it out, He comes in. Do you believe it? Will you do it right now? By yourself? Don't lean on anyone else. Don't trust anyone else. Come only by yourself—alone.

8

CLOUDS
THAT OBSTRUCT

Throughout the previous chapters you may have asked yourself, exactly what is it am I advocating in this book? I would like to clarify my concerns and simply state, my words contain nothing else but Christ. Any spiritual teaching that is not just more of Christ is false. I am most concerned today that all our doctrinal foundations be based on the Scriptures, and its whole spiritual mood be apostolic. It must also be found in harmony with the best in the historic church, the best in devotional literature, the best in hymnody, and the best in biography. Why does this kind of preaching sound different? Why does it sound strange when compared to much of today's so-called true gospel preaching?

A number of years ago, textualism captured the gospel church. By the gospel church I mean the fundamentalist church. I am referring to the gospel church in which people believe in Christ the Savior and accept Him as such. In this church, scribes and lawyers have taken over and set up a hierarchy in schools, Bible conferences, and churches. Many have established the rule of a rigid adherence to words.

I believe and have believed nothing else throughout my entire life but in the plenary, that is, the full, verbal inspiration of the Scriptures as originally given. Let me clarify this by saying I believe and have always believed, as a responsible Christian teacher and believer, in the plenary, verbal inspiration of the Scriptures as originally given.

We find the problem has been and still is that this textual school of thought rests solely on verbal inspiration. In the doctrine of verbal inspiration, rigor mortis has set in, resulting in the religious imagination becoming stultified. This has caused religious yearning to be choked down and religious aspiration slapped down. The longing, aspiring wings of the children of God were clipped like a hen in the hen coop. We have been told to shut up and like what we have. This is it. This has resulted with the language of the New Testament persisting, but the Spirit of the New Testament grieved.

You may wonder how this came about. This came as a result of a revolt, a revolt against the scribes that took two directions. Masses of evangelicals revolted without knowing they were revolting. They didn't know they were gasping as a fish in a bowl void of oxygen. The masses revolted into religious entertainment to the point now where many gospel churches are now camping on the doorstep of the theater. Over against that on the opposite side is where there are the more intelligent fundamentalists and evangelicals who have revolted into evangelical rationalism, and in some cases are already busy making its peace with liberalism.

This is why we don't hear of much of what I am teaching about the deeper spiritual life. I know it sounds strange to hear someone advocating what I do, because on one side we have the masses saying I've accepted Jesus and declaring let's go and have fun, and on the other side there are serious, reverent men thinking their way perilously close to the borders of liberalism. All too often, the New Testament message and its objectives and methods have been allowed to lie dormant. In the name of the lordship of Jesus, which is lordship in name only, we have introduced our own message, our own objectives, and then have thought out our own methods for achieving those objectives. In many cases these fail to be scriptural at all.

Do you think it is heresy to yearn and pray and long after God? Is that heresy? Does it constitute a radical mind to yearn and pray and fight? Can you recall the great prayer I have spoken of in *The Cloud of Unknowing*? "God, I beseech Thee so for to cleanse the intent of mine heart with the unspeakable gift of Thy grace, that I may perfectly love Thee, and worthily praise Thee." We are to long perfectly to love God and worthily to praise Him and to mean more than words when you say it. It means even if it costs you everything. Is that heresy? Should they put a man in jail for it? Should he be ostracized for it in the light of our hymnody and in the light of our devotion books back to Paul, in the light of the biographies of the saints? No, I think not.

In a book called *The Philokalia*, Nicephorus writes wanting to help us as Christians move forward to know God and to do what *The Cloud of Unknowing* called being "oned" with God—united with God. I would like all Bible Christians to ask themselves the question, could I go along with this? Nicephorus was a

Greek Christian. That is, he was in the Greek Orthodox church. He wasn't a Protestant and he wasn't a Roman Catholic and he wasn't a Mar Thoma and he wasn't a Coptic nor a Nestor. He belonged over on the Greek side, but he was a saint. He wrote a little book to help people to go on with God, in which he said, "You, who desire to capture the wondrous divine illumination of our Savior Jesus Christ—who seek to feel the divine fire in your heart." Here was a scholar and a saint who wrote this classic book back in the sixteenth century and is recognized as such. He dared to use the words "who seek to feel the divine fire in your heart" and "strive to sense the experience and feeling of reconciliation with God—who, in order to unearth the treasure buried in the field of your hearts and to gain possession of it, have renounced everything worldly—who desire the candles of your soul to burn brightly even now."

We have become so dispensational-minded that we have pushed everything into the future, but this man says, you "who desire the candles of your soul to burn brightly even now." The apostle Peter said, in this present world and who for this purpose have renounced all this world, who wish by conscious experience—conscious experience; you'd think he was a modern psychologist—to know and to receive the kingdom of heaven existing within you. He said what I have been teaching all the time, that Christ dwells in the heart of every believer. "Know ye not . . . that Jesus Christ is in you, except ye be reprobates?" (2 Cor. 13:5). And "if any man have not the Spirit of Christ, he is none of his" (Rom. 8:9). And the riches of the mind lie potentially there, but we have been forbidden to believe it, or forbidden to say so. And we have been choked down and the oxygen cut off and our wings clipped and our longings chilled. And that's why what I say sounds different and strange. And people say, what is this new doctrine? It's no new doctrine at all.

I would like to highlight now what I call the cloud of concealment. Christ has made full atonement for us. Let's start there. Christ has made full atonement. "Christ has for sin atonement made, what a wonderful Savior!" Would you like to hear it said for you by somebody else that could say it better than the theologians—little Lady Julian? Here's what she said: "The precious amends, or satisfaction our Lord hath made for man's sin, turning all our blame into endless honor." Could it be said sweeter than that? The precious amends our Lord hath made for man's sin, turning all our blame into endless honor. Paul said it a little differently. He said, where sin abounded, grace does *what*? It much more abounds, turning all our blame into endless honor (Rom. 5:20–21).

God's face is turned toward us. Think deeply on that. Don't let the devil deceive you. Don't let doubt assail you. Don't let anything I or others say cheat you from the glorious knowledge that the face of God is turned toward you. As a Christian, the smiling face of God is always turned toward you. Why then do we not enjoy? Let's look again at these words. Why then do we as Christians not capture the wondrous, divine illumination of the Savior, Jesus Christ? Why do we not feel the divine fire in our hearts? Why do we not strive to sense and experience, or better yet, why do we not sense and experience the feeling of reconciliation with God as well as the knowledge of it? And why do we not gain possession of it?

Oh, I know this is often dismissed by saying your position

and your possession, but that can get so cold as dry ice. Why is it the candles of our soul do not burn more brightly even now? Why is it we don't have the conscious experience and know and receive the kingdom existing within us? It is because between us and the smiling face of God lies a cloud of concealment.

Consider for a moment with me that there is no such a thing as a day when the sun doesn't shine. A newspaper in Florida offered to give all of one day's run of their newspaper free of charge if the sun doesn't shine somewhere. Let me state the obvious. The sun shines every day, and there has never been a day from the hour God told the sun to rule the day that the sun hasn't shone.

We all have to acknowledge the existence of dark days and misty days and cloudy days and days when it gets so dark you have to turn on the lights, and so dark in the country that the chickens go to roost. I've seen it. Despite these occasional dark days, the sun is still shining just as brightly as on the brightest, clearest day in June. Why then does it not shine on the earth? It is because between the sun and the earth is a cloud of concealment. The sun, though concealed, is all right. It's up there grinning broadly and just as bright and just as hot and just as radiant as ever, but its brightness doesn't get through to the earth because there is a cloud of concealment.

What is this cloud? We understand this from the standpoint of weather, but what is it as spiritually applied to Christians, and what really is the matter? It's the cloud of concealment, a cloud that we allow to be over us as Christians. And what is this cloud, considering atonement has been made and there is nothing to do, for it's all been done? For you, not a drop of blood needs to be shed. Not a spear needs to enter a holy heart. Not a tear nor a groan or a drop of sweat. Not a moment in agony. Death has no more dominion over Him. It is done! It is finished! It is forever done! The face of God shines down upon us. What is this cloud upon Christians, that is, above Christians? "There's a cloud of concealment betwixt thee and thy God," *The Cloud of Unknowing* says. What is that cloud? Well, it's a cloud that may be one thing or it may be many things.

For instance, there is the cloud of pride. You are your Father's child and heaven is your home, and yet for a lifetime you may go without the wondrous, divine illumination of the Savior, Jesus Christ; without feeling the divine fire in your heart or sensing or experiencing the feeling of reconciliation with God. You are living without the candles of your soul burning brightly, because you have allowed a cloud of pride to hang over your head. The devil will tell you that God hates you. God has turned His back on you. The devil lies.

The back of God has never been turned to a child of God nor a repentant sinner since the hour Jesus groaned and died and said, "It is finished." The face of God is always turned our way. But we allow this cloud of pride and the cloud of stubbornness. There are some people that are just plain stubborn. They will not bend. They will not yield, neither to man nor God nor to anybody except the law and death; they just won't. This is a cloud of stubbornness as when God complained about Israel when He said, your neck is brass and your forehead is hard. He couldn't get them to yield.

Next, there is the cloud of self-will. Self-will is a very religious thing. It may become religious and get converted and enter right along with you into the church when you join and go in with you into the chamber when you pray, yet it is self-will. Self-will is only good-natured when it gets its own way, and is grouchy and ill-tempered when it is cross. Think about that. Is your surrender to God sufficient so that you can be spiritual even when you're cross?

And then there's ambition. Did you know there's even religious ambition? There are people who are religiously ambitious for perhaps something that isn't in the will of God or that is for self-aggrandizement, leading to a cloud forming above them between them and their God. Here's an amusing little proverb in the Knox translation that reads like this. It rather amuses me because it's so true and it is such a perfect picture of the human heart. He says, "Tripped by his own folly, a man eats his heart out, finding fault with the Lord." You will find Christians like that, tripped by their own folly. They eat their heart out finding fault even with God, having what God calls a controversy with me.

Another cloud of concealment is in everything I claim for myself. This is the one thing I have long preached about which I suppose is hard for some Christians to grasp—that I've got to give up everything. For instance, my own pastoral position must go on the block, and I must be ready at any moment to give it up and let it ride away on any sermon I preach or any position I take. I dare not stick to it. My job as the editor of the *Alliance Weekly* magazine, or my position in the religious world—everything has to be on the block and ready to go! If I own it, it is a cloud over my head and it becomes a cloud of obscurity that nothing will penetrate.

People will try to pray through this, but you can't pray

through a cloud of concealment. Nothing can penetrate it. You can try to fast through it. There are people that fast for days out of nothing but stubbornness. History shows us around the world of some who have fasted and even died for political reasons out of just sheer, downright stubbornness. Those who try to fast their way through will find it futile. You can't do it, friend.

A cloud of concealment in your life could possibly be something that you say is yours, but you won't give it up. You think you do, but you don't. There will be a veil over it, and if there's any sun, it will not be very bright. There will be a cloud and you can't pray through it. This idea that if you just pray long enough, everything will be all right. Did you know God has gotten some people up off their knees and told them to quit? There were two different instances when the Lord stopped prayer meetings. Did you know that? He said, it's no use. There was the man Samuel who prayed and prayed. God came and put His hand over his mouth and said, Samuel, don't pray any longer for Saul. He's through. Don't pray for him, and God shut him up.

There was also another instance where Joshua was lying face-down praying. We would have written a tract about him. We would have said, "Oh, what a saint!" But God says, what's the use of lying there on your stomach? I don't honor a man for lying on his belly. Get up on your feet and deal with the situation in your crowd, and then I'll bless you and save you all that lying around and groaning.

So remember this modern idea that if you pray long enough, everything will be okay. The idea that I can hang on to things and then pray the cloud away while I'm hanging on to the cloud. No, you can't do it. The saint of God, though, understands he has to let things go, and then after long seasons of prayer, God will give an answer to your prayer. Prayer is the soul's sincere desire and the breath of the saint and all that I believe in and I think and practice in some measure.

Fear is yet another cloud of concealment. Fear is always a child of unbelief. No matter what you are afraid of, whether it's cancer, or whether there is a possibility your child will get sick, or whether you are likely to lose your job, always remember: fear is a child of unbelief. And fear over your head is a cloud of obscurity and hides that smiling Face from you. It doesn't turn the Face away, for the blood of atonement keeps His face forever turned toward His people and toward repentant sinners.

Next is self-love. We make a joke out of this, but we should never make a joke out of it, friend, because self-love is a cloud of concealment—a cloud of obscurity. Even the Christian who has offered himself to Christ and has believed and is converted can keep a cloud of concealment over him simply by loving himself. And to fall out of love with yourself is an accident. I don't mean an accident like falling off of something, but rather abnormal not to love yourself.

Related to self-love is self-congratulation and self-admiration. These self-sins are there and will remain there. The odd thing about these self-sins is the scribes of today have excused them and proved they should be there, and therefore we can't do anything about it. Yet, we cry within us, oh, that the candles of my soul might burn brightly, even now. Oh, that I might know the divine illumination of my Savior, Jesus Christ. And we groan with a groan that goes back to Paul in Philippians. It goes back to David in the Psalms, that we might come into a warm, personal, present, and lasting fellowship with Jesus Christ that lifts us and irradiates our hearts. We can't because we admire ourselves and we're not going to have anybody disturb us. We either congratulate ourselves or we love ourselves.

May I add money to our list of clouds? Money these days gets "betwixt thee and thy God," as the old brother calls it. It gets betwixt thee and thy God. Some evangelist years ago in my hearing pointed out that you can take two dimes and shut out a landscape. You can take two dimes with you to the Great Smoky Mountains, go clear to the top knob of the great Smokies, and with two dimes shut out all the glorious, green, rolling, blue cap vista of the Great Smokies. Just put them in front of your eyes and put them close enough. That's all it takes. The mountains are still there smiling in the sun, but you don't see them because there's a dime in front of each eye. It doesn't really take much money. Some who don't have much money often make snide remarks about the rich man. You can be rich and still have only ten dollars. If it gets between you and your God, that cloud is concealing God from you.

And then there are people, just plain people. The Lord tells us that we shouldn't be afraid of man with his breath in his nostrils. Yet, there are people who are Christians who have a cloud of fear above them, a constant cloud of fear. They want to fit in with society. The sociologists tell us we must do this. We must adjust to society. Schools are busy, but instead of teaching history and writing and reading and arithmetic and all the rest, they're teaching children to adjust so as not to be odd and just get along with others. If that is your goal, you have a cloud over your heart, my Christian friend.

Another cloud of concealment is our friends, and then there's the position we hold, whatever it may be. Our loved ones can obscure our view of God. This is the tenderest and perhaps the hardest, but it's all got to go.

You may ask then, "What do I do with this, if this cloud is over my head and has become a cloud of concealment? My Father is smiling at me, but I can't see His face. What shall I do?" Well, the old brother in *The Cloud of Unknowing* suggests, and I borrow it as well, a beautiful illustration. He calls it a cloud of forgetting. He said, "Put this cloud that's above you under your feet as a cloud of forgetting." Paul said exactly the same thing: "Forgetting those things which are behind, and reaching forth unto those things which are before" (Phil. 3:13).

You see, the things which were behind Paul were a cloud, and if they had been in front of him, they would have shut out God. He put them behind himself: his defeats, his mistakes, his blunders, his errors, his wrongs, the times he'd fallen on his face, and the time the Lord had to rebuke him for his pride. All this he put behind him and under his feet as a cloud of forgetting. And *The Cloud of Unknowing* says you should put them under you and not have them betwixt thee and thy God. Rightly so, "put a cloud of forgetting beneath thee, betwixt thee and all the creatures that ever God made." We have got to get that cloud of forgetting under our feet.

That's the job of the Christian. And that's why I'm teaching like this. Some people understand this and are going to do something about it. Others are not. Others have come up to their Kadesh Barnea once a week for years and have turned back into the wilderness and wonder why there is sand in their shoes. It's because you would not go on to Kadesh Barnea. Rightly so, put a cloud of forgetting beneath yourself and all this that had been a cloud of concealment. It now becomes a cloud of forgetting.

All the while, the face of God is still smiling, and none of the clouds I've mentioned, and no other clouds the devil might blow up, will change God. The devil can blow up a storm and put it in between you and the face of your God experientially. Remember, though, God is waiting within the veil. Or to change the figure, He's waiting for you to move up.

I remember getting on a plane at LaGuardia in New York some years ago. It was about three o'clock in the afternoon. The smiling and relaxed friendly pilot came out and made a little speech. He knew that old duffers like me would worry about the flight because it was raining miserably that day, just plain miserable. He told us we were going to leave in a moment, but in about fifteen minutes we would be up in the sunlight—only fifteen minutes to see sunlight. He went on to say the weather reports showed clear skies from New York to Chicago. So, we got into that plane almost feeling our way through the heavy smog, and in fifteen minutes we put the cloud under our feet with the bright shining sun above us. As we rose, even the clouds became white beneath us.

If you have flown a lot, you most likely have had the same experience of seeing those great billows of whipped cream that are underneath you, as white as whipped eggs. When you're underneath them and look up, they look like a misty, miserable, smoggy thing that has shut out the sun. But in minutes, you can put them under your feet. Isn't it nice to take off in the smoke and rain and fly nine hundred miles all the way home in the sunshine?

Now, that's what I mean. You are going to have to put these clouds under your feet. You're going to have to get intentional and do something more than just sit and take in some more. You're going to have to work on yourself. Oh, there are those who have every excuse in the world. They're just not going up. They'd rather stay right down here in the smog while the sun shines brightly above the clouds. They think the sun isn't shining when in fact it is. Put it all under you, my friend; put it all under you.

What are these clouds? They are money, people, friends, position, loved ones, fear, all that I claim and call my own, ambitions, pride, stubbornness, self-will, and anything else the Holy Spirit may point to in your life. Only you know what it is. He is a jealous lover, and He suffereth no rival. Whatever the rival is, it's a cloud between you and God. I am not saying you aren't joined to Him. I am not saying you are not justified. What I am saying is this wondrous, divine illumination, this ability to perfectly love Him and worthily to praise Him has been choked out, smitten down, and taught out of us for generations. This we lack, and we lack it because we will not put under our feet the cloud of obscurity. We let it rise between us and our God.

Friend, if you will put it underneath you, you will find that it hides all the past and everything that has bothered you and that which has shamed you and now worries you and grieves you. It's down there and it's out and it's gone and there's nothing left but the clear sky above. If you have put the cloud under you, then "He wills thou do but look on Him and let Him alone."

A. B. Simpson once wrote a song no one sings anymore for at least a couple of reasons. One is that the tune is bad. The second is that it describes the experience that far too few possess. The song says,

> I clasp the hand of love divine,
> I claim the gracious promise mine,
> And this eternal countersign,
> "I take"—"He undertakes."

> I take Thee, blessed Lord,
> I give myself to Thee;
> And Thou, according to Thy word,
> Dost undertake for me.

Christ doesn't have to die again. No cross needs ever to be erected again. No value needs to be added to the atonement.

The face of God smiles on His people, but the clouds hide Him—your cloud and my cloud. You say, that's true of sinners. That's true of backsliders. But that couldn't be true of good gospel people. It is true of the masses of the people. And because that cloud has been above them, and because they've been taught they can't rise, they rush to get a little heartbeat from the theater, rush to get a little bit of warmth, the feeling from a hillbilly ballad singing religious songs and theatrics and all the rest. I don't blame them. They have been cheated and the legalists have wronged them as in the days of Jesus. Jesus walked among men in that day with His eyes bright and His vision keen. And He said to them, whatever they tell you, do, because they're theologically right, but don't be like them. And they said, we'll kill that man, and they did kill that man. But He rose on the third day and sent down the Holy Spirit into the world. And He's mine and yours, our sweet possession.

Don't let anybody tell you how much you can have of Him. Only God can tell you how much you can have of Him. Don't you let anybody take you aside and tell you not to get excited and not to get fanatical. Don't let them tell you that you possess all there is. Don't you let that happen to you. Just as sure as God lives, if we continue in the direction we've been moving in evangelical and gospel circles, that which is now fundamentalism will in a short time be liberalism. We have got to have the Holy Spirit back. We've got to have the face of God shining down and the candles of our souls burning bright. We need to once again sense and feel and know the wondrous, divine illumination of Him who said, I'm the light of the world.

Many Christians have been walking around under a cloud for a long time. You can't get above it, you just can't, because you've tried to pray your way above it. You have tried to believe your way above it, but it doesn't work that way. It can't. You've got to put it under your feet and rise above it and put all these things betwixt thee and all the creatures God ever made and look away to the sunlight. Then you will be able to relax, for there's nothing you can do.

What can a man do? He can't fill himself with the Holy Spirit. He can't cleanse his own heart. You and I can't crucify ourselves. We can't. God has to do it, and He will do it. He waits to do it. He waits, optimistic and friendly. He's on your side wanting to help you, willing to do, anxious to do it, if we can use the word *anxious* as touching God. But we sit back and we're discouraged and we're blue. And we've been to so many altars and we've read so many books, and we're all confused, yet the sun shines, and still the cloud hovers. And yet, God's poor people won't crowd it under their feet.

"Into the sunshine in fifteen minutes," said the pilot. "Into the sunshine in fifteen minutes," says the man of God to you right now if you'll put it all under your feet. Dare to put it under your feet and look away to the Lord Jesus, not trying to tell Him what to do nor how to do it. Look on Him and let Him work. And over the next hours and days and weeks, you will move upward into a place of spiritual restfulness and power such as you have never known before, and you will have a marvelous deliverance from bondage, a marvelous freedom. You will believe in the Scriptures. You will believe in the Word of God and its verbal inspiration, its full plenary importance. You'll believe in it, and yet out of it there will come a fragrance and a radiance and illumination which you have never dreamed of before.

Do you think there could be any valid objection to that raised by anyone? If I had thought anybody could raise a valid objection, I wouldn't ask. The New Testament teaches that the Lord's people met and prayed together. They prayed for each other. The strong ones prayed for the weak ones and the ones that had fallen. The others prayed for them and helped them. In one instance, they met and prayed together and the place was shaken and they were all filled with the Holy Spirit. That's in the book too. That's in the Bible. That is, until it was ruled away and said it couldn't be for us today.

The blessed Holy Dove was forced to fold His wings and be quiet while the saints that believed it and radiated in the joy of it lived in it for years gone by. Today, we've been told to be quiet.

The scribes have told us what to believe about this. But our own hungry hearts tell us the scribes are wrong, and our longing souls tell us the hymn writers and the devotional writers and those of whose biographies we have read—they were right.

9

OBSTACLES IN OUR WAY

The apostle Paul famously states in Philippians 3 those things which were gain to him he counted as loss for Christ. He only wanted to be found in Him, not having his own righteousness, but the righteousness which is of God through faith, or by faith. He said, "If by any means I might attain. . . . Not as though I had already attained, either were already perfect: but I follow after" (Phil. 3:11–12). I forget the things that are behind and I press forward. And let us therefore as many as be perfect be thus minded.

This man, this most aggressive man, this bold man, this surest-footed man, and this saintliest man, moved by the Holy Spirit said in Acts that in every city, "bonds and afflictions abide me. But none of these things move me, neither count I my life dear unto myself, so that I might finish my course with joy" (Acts 20:23–24). In 1 Corinthians 4:15–16, he said rather tartly, "Though ye have ten thousand instructors in Christ, yet have ye not many fathers: for in Christ Jesus I have begotten you through the gospel. Wherefore I beseech you, be ye followers of me." In 1 Corinthians again, fifth chapter, he said, "I . . . have judged already, as though I were present, concerning him that hath so done this deed, in the name of our Lord Jesus Christ . . . deliver such an one unto Satan for the destruction of the flesh, that the spirit may be saved in the day of the Lord Jesus." In Galatians 6:17 he said, "From henceforth let no man trouble me: for I bear in my body the marks of the Lord Jesus."

Now, those are only five texts, but you'll find them all through Acts and the Epistles. There was a surefootedness about the man Paul. None of this crawling around on his tummy. This man knew what he believed. He knew where he stood. He knew God and he was confident with a great cosmic confidence. But that same man was yet the most self-distrustful man, because in 1 Corinthians 15:9–10 he said, "For I am the least of the apostles, that am not meet to be called an apostle. . . . But by the grace of God I am what I am." He continues in 2 Corinthians, "But we have this treasure in earthen vessels, that the excellency of the power may be of God, and not of us" (2 Cor. 4:7). Then in 1 Timothy 1:15 he says, "This is a faithful saying, and worthy of all acceptation, that Christ Jesus came into the world to save sinners; of whom I am chief." And in Romans 7:18 he says, "For I know that in me (that is, in my flesh,) dwelleth no good thing."

Please understand, I haven't exhausted these texts; I've only given you four or five proof texts on each side. Therefore, we may properly conclude that Paul's great personal triumph resulted from an entire and radical distrust of himself. Self-trust is our last great obstacle to spiritual triumph. Paul just didn't trust himself. Before men, he was bold as a lion. Before God He couldn't say too much against himself. Rather, he had no confidence in himself at all, and the confidence of the man in God was in inverse proportion to his confidence in himself. As far as he trusted himself, he did not trust God. As far as he distrusted himself, he was thrown out upon God.

Self-trust, respectability, and self-assurance which come by education, birth, what you hear about yourself, and what your friends tell you about yourself, are the last great obstacles to go out of the Christian's life. As I shall explain, after we think it's gone, it still isn't gone. And that is why we wait around the deep river of God as animals around the waterhole, afraid to go in, and we never do quite go in.

There was an old man by the name of Lorenzo Scupoli that I want to quote a little. He had a wonderful name. I think Lorenzo Scupoli was one of those strange Protestants who, during his lifetime, fought a running fight and was considered (more or less) a heretic because of his evangelical views. It was way back four hundred years ago when he said, "Distrust of yourself is so necessary to you in this combat, that without it, you must hold it certain." What I like about such men as this and Paul and others is the clear, sharp language they use. He said, this distrust of yourself is so necessary to you in this spiritual combat that without it, you must hold it certain that you will not be able to attain the desired victory—distrust of self.

Scupoli goes on to say, "We are much too easily inclined by our corrupt nature to a false opinion of ourselves." Without any foundation at all, he says, we presume vainly in our own strength.

He continues to describe this false opinion of ourselves as "a defect very difficult to understand and most displeasing in the eyes of God who loves us and desires in us a loyal recognition that every grace and every virtue proceeds from Him alone who is the fountain of all good, and that nothing, not even a good thought, can come from us, except it be of His will."

In our evangelical culture today, you can be converted, born again, and be walking around testifying for a hundred years and never find this out. And most of us haven't been around a hundred years, and we still haven't found this out yet. We haven't found out what Paul found, and what we glibly quote—but it never reaches us—this major obstacle to spiritual victory is self-trust.

After sin has been put away (that is, every sin that we know has been put away in our search for God), and after all the self-sins we know of have been crucified and we've stopped boasting, we've stopped loving ourselves and we think we have put away the hyphenated self-sins, and think they're pretty well gone; and we've reckoned ourselves indeed to be dead and have died unto sin through Jesus Christ; and even after we've humbled ourselves, even publicly by going to an altar, then self-trust may be stronger than it was before, because you see, it has more foundation to build on.

And so, after we have put away our sins, and after we have given up our wealth, and after we have taken the poor position and allowed ourselves to be shoved around, and after noses have been rubbed in the dust, then self-trust whispers its consolation. A lot of people mistake that consolation of self-whispering for the Holy Spirit, and that's why we're so weak when we think we're strong. Self-consolation, or self-trust, whispers like this. It says, "Now you're far in advance of others."

When you feel far in advance of others and have put your sin behind you, and you've confessed and humbled yourself, "you may trust yourself, of course with God's help," says self, "and you may expect the victory to come and power to be at your side. You're not one of these dead ones. You're one of these live ones," self tells you. "It has cost you a lot, hasn't it?" So, self gently rubs your back downwards, and you enjoy it so much. And self says, "You've put your sin behind you, haven't you? Yes. And you've humbled yourself. You're getting somewhere. Of course, you understand it has got to be God's help."

That's self-trust. And almost all the joy the average Christian has is the back scratching self gives him. All the pleasure he gets is the back scratching he gets from self. We take a cat and scratch it between the ears and it'll close its eyes. We used to call it "hunker down" back in Pennsylvania. Do you know what hunkering down means? *Hunkering* is an old Scotch word that means crouching. A cat will crouch because they love to be scratched. A cow will come and put her head over the fence and if you scratch it between the ears and pat her head, she'll love it and stand there.

Self is always scratching the ears of the people of God. The further they go on into the will of God and the deeper they go, the more back-scratching they get. And self says, "Well, certainly you know better. You've read Thomas à Kempis and you're different. You love the old hymns, and you're a separated Christian. None of this crazy modern stuff is for you. You're better." And you don't know that is happening to you. You're feeling good.

"You're feeling good" is strictly being scratched by a self that hasn't yet died. There is the self-trust that you thought was gone.

Why is self-trust so wrong? Self-trust is so wrong because it robs God to give to man. It takes away from God the ultimate, final trust. It misjudges God and man, and holds God to be less than He is and man to be more than he is. And this is mainly the trouble with us. We think God is less than He is and man is more than he is. We can go to school and study theology and learn how God is the source and fountain and all the rest, and then learn about His attributes, and still in our hearts believe God is less than He is and we are more than we are.

Consider the moon. Suppose the moon could talk and think and have a personality. What if the moon should say, "Well, I shine on the earth. And every time that I am around where I can reach the earth, I see the earth becomes beautiful." Someone could say, "Don't you know that by yourself, you're burned ash? Don't you know that you've been discovered and found out you don't shine at all? You only reflect the sun's light. It's the sun that shines."

I could see self telling the moon, "Well, you're letting your light shine and you're doing a good job. I noticed when you're not up the whole side of the earth lies in darkness, but when you come it lightens up and you begin to see the rooms of houses and you do a fine job." The moon would nod and say, "Well, the glory belongs to God, and by the grace of God, I'm like this." But all the time, the moon thinks it's shining when the moon isn't shining at all. It's reflecting. The apostle Paul could boldly shine and talk about it because he knew he wasn't shining at all. He knew he didn't have a thing that was fit for heaven. It was the grace of

God in him. And he knew it was God and not he. He completely and radically distrusted himself.

No man ever really knows about himself. He doesn't know how weak he is. No man really comprehends what he sounds like. Everyone thinks his voice sounds good until he hears himself on a recording. One of the most humbling things that ever happened to me was when I heard my first sermon recording. After hearing it, I haven't been able to stand it since. I may not be able to stand the sound of my own voice, but the recording doesn't lie. Up to that time, I had been told I had a fine preaching voice. People commented, "Good voice." But I heard it.

No one knows the sound of their own voice until they hear it. And no one knows how weak they are until God has exposed them. Nobody wants to be exposed, but God has to expose you. And what we consider our strength is actually our weakness. If you will think over your life reverently and carefully in prayer and put down on a pad the things you think are your virtues, those are your weaknesses; and those very virtues are your sources of trouble. The only way you can deal with yourself is to look away and look unto Him, as I've been saying. You have to simply stop thinking about yourself at all.

No one can really know how weak he is, and no one can know how bad he is until he has been exposed by the Holy Spirit. No one wants to be exposed and shown how he unstable is. Do you remember the fellow Hazael in the Old Testament book of 2 Kings who said, "Is thy servant a dog, that he should do this great thing?" (2 Kings 8:13). Apparently, he meant it and went straight home and did it. The prophet said, you're going to murder your master. He said, "Is thy servant a dog?"

The prophet didn't reply, but he went home and put a pillow over his master's face and smothered him to death.

Do you remember a certain great, old, bold fisherman who stood up and said, "Let everybody else run from you, Lord; I'll not!" The Lord said before the cock crows twice, you will. And he did. You will find that no one really knows how unstable he is. And that's why it's dangerous to trust our good habits. That's why it's dangerous to trust our virtue, because we're unstable.

How then do we learn self-distrust? There are four ways that God teaches distrust. There may be some others, but these four are valid ways. *The Cloud of Unknowing* writer tells us it's the work of God's hand, this distrust. And what he says is supported and confirmed by almost all of the devotional writers and the great humanists or persons about whom biographies have been written. He says sometimes it comes by holy inspiration, which I believe to be the best way to get it. The best way to find out you're no good is to have God flash a holy inspiration into your soul and just let you know suddenly. I think that's happened to some people.

Nicholas Herman, who was called Brother Lawrence, said it happened to him. He said he was never once out of the presence of God in forty years, never out of the conscious presence of God. He said, "When I took the cross and decided to obey Jesus and walk this holy way, from reading around and hearing, I gathered that I have to suffer a lot." But he said, "For some reason, God never counted me worthy of much suffering. He just let me continue to trust Him. I put all my self-trust away, and I'm trusting in God completely." Paraphrasing it, he was carrying his cross. He said he believed God was in him and around him and near him as he was praying all the time. Brother Lawrence said, "He's never given me very much suffering to do."

Throughout my ministry, I have spoken about little old Lady Julian, and many are now searching for her books and all the rest. She only wrote one book. And outside of that one experience she had when she received her three wounds, she never had to do much suffering. God gave her by a holy inspiration a light to her heart, and she knew instantly she was no good and Jesus Christ was everything, and she stayed right there in her belief until she died, growing every day.

The easiest way to get self-distrust would be for the Lord to just come in by a sweet sudden holy inspiration within our hearts through the Scriptures and tell us how bad we are. You can be a confirmed believer in total depravity and be as proud as Lucifer and trust yourself so as to shut out the face of God and prevent victory. Theological total depravity isn't what's meant here at all. I happen to be one of those who believes according to the Scriptures that man is an alien by birth and a sinner by choice. I have never believed anything else. I have never had any trouble with theology.

Over the years, I have received letters from people writing about their difficulties with theology. I either don't have sense enough or the dear Lord preserves me, because I have never had a worry or care about total depravity, or that I have inherited evil from my father. I don't know a thing about it. All I know is, as soon as I was big enough to sin, I went into the business. And I know that every child I've ever known or seen did the same thing.

No matter who you are, every race and every nationality have their vices, don't they? Everybody, every nationality, everyone has his own vice. But there is one vice that stands out. God knows there may be a thousand, but at least one stands out, because we're all alike. We're born bad. And we can believe that and accept it and teach it boldly to others. And those who mostly trust themselves may yet be the ones who are often quoted. All our righteousness is but filthy rags. I am careful to put the *s* on the end to confirm the fact that it's not just singular, but is plural. Our righteousness is filthy rags.

Now, you see it takes the Holy Spirit to tell you you're bad and make you see it. It takes the Holy Spirit to tell you you're weak and make you see it. The teacher can tell you you're weak, and you can go through and get a degree and yet come out and still go proudly out to be a preacher or probably out to be a missionary or a Bible teacher. But Paul says God is wont to give His friends, to tell His Jewish friends and teach them self-distrust, sometimes with holy inspiration or secondly, sometimes with harsh scourges. That's more where I come in. Sometimes with harsh scourges.

I don't know whom we could use for a better illustration than the man Job. We so pity Job with human sympathy. And we sort of half take Job's part against God if we don't watch ourselves. We can certainly take Job's part against his wife. The only good thing I know about her was that she was never heard of again. I don't know what happened to her, but she got out of the picture. But have you noticed this man Job was a long way from being a humble man? Did you ever notice that? He was a praying man. And he was a man who had made sacrifices lest his children had sinned the night before at their party. He couldn't keep them from having the party, but he could go to God on his knees and pray for them, and he did.

Listen to Job toward the latter third of his long talk. He said,

> Oh that I were as in months past, as in the days when God preserved me; when his candle shined upon my head, and when by his light I walked through darkness; as I was in the days of my youth, when the secret of God was upon my tabernacle; when the Almighty was yet with me, when my children were about me; when I washed my steps with butter, and the rock poured me out rivers of oil; when I went out to the gate through the city, when I prepared my seat in the street! (Job 29:2–7)

Job was considered a big shot in his day because that is what they did then. They didn't have a city hall. There was a place at the head of the street where all the big shots sat. Job said, "The young men saw me, and hid themselves: and the aged arose, and stood up" (Job 29:8). Who's this coming down the street? The honorable Mr. Job. Oh, he said, here I am lying now in this ash pile, a miserable wreck. They have cast me out, and nobody would vote for me. And he said that the day was when he went down the street, the young people hid themselves and the old people stood up. And princes refrained from talking and laid their hands on their mouth.

Do you think Brother Job was an ordinary rag picker? Brother Job was a great man and he knew it, and that was the trouble. That's why he had to have all that happen to him. If you're great and don't know it, nothing will happen to you. But if you happen to suspect it, and you love God, things will start to happen to you. And if they don't, it's because you're not far enough along for the Lord to trust you yet. He said, "The nobles held their peace, and their tongue cleaved to the roof of their mouth. When the ear heard me, then it blessed me; and when the eye saw me, it gave witness to me: because I delivered the poor that cried, and the fatherless, and him that had none to help him. The blessing of him that was ready to perish came upon me" (Job 29:10–13). That was Job. He was just telling them of the kind of fellow he used to be. And the awful part about this is, it was only a half-prayer.

Job had been there on the ash pile for I don't know how long with these enemies all around him. God, though, went on until the harsh circumstances took root and discouragement began to bite into the soul of the man. Finally, the time came when he said, O God, I've been talking and talking and talking, but now I'll shut up. I'll put my hand over my mouth. I am vile, O God. And when he got that lesson the Lord said, all right, Job, now pray for the rest of them. So, he prayed for the rest of them. And God gave him back twice as much.

Nobody wants to hear anything about our dear Heavenly Father being wont to teach His children distrust by harsh scourgings. Some might think I'm a hard man, that I like to lay on the lash. On the contrary; if I could, I'd preach on the Twenty-Third Psalm every Sunday for a year. Then after I was through with the Twenty-Third Psalm, I'd take up the fifty-third chapter of Isaiah. And finished with that, I would preach on 1 Corinthians 13. If I did that, though, do you know where you'd be in the meantime? You would be among the spongiest, softest Christians around.

God has to give us harsh scourgings sometimes. It would be like feeding your family nothing but sugar cookies. Do you know what would happen to them? They'd lose their teeth by the time they were twelve years old. There has to be some solid stuff. The harsh scourgings, we talk about it briefly and pass it by. Nobody puts any emphasis there.

The third way is sometimes with violent and insuperable temptation. When we're violently tempted, and for a moment insuperably tempted, we're inclined to throw in the white towel and say, "God, it's no use. It's no use. I'm no good. I have read about Moody and Augustine and all the rest, but it's no use, God. You don't want me. I'm finished," forgetting all the while that God wants to teach His friends self-distrust, sometimes by violent and insuperable temptations. And sometimes when something blows up in you that you thought was dead, you take it as a proof that you're not a Christian, when you ought to take it as a proof that you are nearer home today than you were yesterday, and that your heavenly Father is letting this thing happen to you to show you you are indeed good.

Now, back to Brother Lawrence. He said that he walked with the Lord all the time, but he said, if ever I make a slip anywhere, I never let it give me much trouble. I go straight to the Lord and I say, now Lord, that's me, and if You don't help me, that's what You can expect, for that's me. Then he said, God forgave me and I went right on from there.

We are told sometimes by men that repentance is a long-drawn-out affair where we have to beat ourselves a long time. But there comes a time when we realize that the best way to handle sin is to do as Fénelon said—the best repentance is turn toward God and don't do it anymore. That's the best repentance in this world. If you did something last week that you're ashamed of and under conviction and condemnation, you should ask yourself how you can repent. The best repentance is to turn to the Lord, tell Him, and then don't do it anymore. That's the best repentance in the wide world.

Are temptations that let you fall down sometimes proof that you're not a true Christian at all? No. They are proof that your conscience is tender and you are very near to God, and that the Lord is trying to teach you that last lesson of self-distrust by a violent temptation. Do you remember Jacob's temptations? And how about Peter's and many others' as well, all down the years?

There is a fourth way our heavenly Father wants to teach us self-distrust by other means that are not understood by us. Sometimes, God teaches you self-distrust by methods in which you don't know what's happening to you. In other words, what God uses, you don't know what they are. You're a Christian, you know it and you love God and you're sick of all the nonsense in the world and you're sick of all the nonsense in the church. Your heart is crying after God as the roe after the water brook, and your heart and your flesh cries out for God, even the living God. And yet, here's this obstacle. You still trust yourself. You're born again. You can say that and testify to it. You love your Bible. You have your prayer, and you're a good Christian. But you still trust yourself.

God still picks us up and carries us and makes all our beds in our sickness and understands our thoughts and knows we're but dust, yet He is loving and patient toward us. And so, God isn't judging. God isn't angry. God is just wanting His children to grow, and sometimes He has to give them some harsh scourging.

What are we to do? Well, we're to trust Him and love Him and absolutely count on Him. Do you know anyone whom you can count on completely? You say to yourself, "Well, let me see . . . would Brother so on and so forth? Do you suppose I could count on him?" Well, do you know anybody you could count on if you were wrong? We can all count on our friends if we are right, but suppose we were in the wrong? Do you know anybody you can count on?

A great old French preacher once said, my friends would fill this great cathedral, but my real friends could occupy these seats here. Now, he wasn't a cynic. He was a realist. Do you know anybody you can count on when you're not right? I can tell you of someone. His name is Jesus. And God has made this same Jesus Lord and Christ.

What you have to do is trust Him completely and let Him work. Don't push Him. Don't struggle. Don't beat the bench and say, "God, You've got to do it now." If you're in the hands of God and obeying God, God is leading you, and you can know absolutely that God will never let you down. He will never, never let you down. Friend, the greatest thing we can possibly do is to see Jesus high and lifted up and know that He's there triumphant, our Brother and Friend who wants to help us, if He can just get our cooperation.

10

KNOWING HIM FULLY

I believe God created the heaven and the earth and all things that are therein. I believe that He made all living creatures and He made each one with a kind of life peculiar to it, the kind of life He chose for it. He then adjusted that kind of life to an environment which He chose for it. As long as each living creature stays in its own environment and lives the kind of life God gave it, that creature fulfills the purpose for which it was made. And God being who He is, nothing higher can be said of any creature than this. He fulfilled that for which God made him.

Many men are honored with their names on the walls of famous buildings. Others have been given prizes of all sorts, such as Nobel Prizes, Pulitzer Prizes and every other kind of prize. You can even canonize them if you wish, but when it's all been said and done, you cannot say any more of a creature than this: God made him and gave him a certain kind of life and has given him an environment to inhabit. And he has lived in that environment with relaxed confidence and has lived the kind of life God gave him. Angels and archangels and seraphim and cherubim and saints and apostles and prophets can't go any further than that.

In the book of Jude, it says the angels which kept not their first estate, but left their own habitation, God hath reserved in everlasting chains under darkness unto the judgment of the Great Day. Here we see a certain order of being, or a certain number of beings of an order that left their first estate. That is, they left the place for which they had been created, and anyone, anybody, any intelligent creature, any moral creature anywhere that leaves its proper sphere and state will know only endless defeat and pain, because they're not fulfilling the end for which they were created. This I say generally of any living being anywhere.

Many are willingly poverty stricken because they're afraid to use their religious imagination and believe what the Bible teaches us. The Bible talks about angels and archangels and the seraphim and cherubim and watchers and holy ones and principalities and powers, yet you and I insist on people only. We are afraid to rise and let our faith-filled imagination encompass the wonder of the filled universe—filled with beings. God created man in His own image, and of no other creature is this spoken.

I cannot find anywhere in the Scriptures where God has said He ever created a seraph in His image, nor a cherub with all of his faces and wings, nor an angel or archangel or principality or power. But it says that God made man in His image. God said affectionately, "Let us make man in our image." So, in the image of God created He him and blew into him the breath of life, and man became a living soul. This may seem radical, but as originally created, man was more like God than any other created creature. As originally created, man was more like God, because of no other creature did God say that He made them in His own image.

A wise old German Christian once said there is nothing in the universe so much like God as the human soul. Of course, he took for granted and meant that man's soul was sinful and lost. And in that sense, sin is not like God, and the soul that sinneth, it shall die. But there is something basic in human nature and in the soul of man that can become more like God than anything else in the universe. I wish we could believe that. I wish we could accept that as a part of our creed and not be afraid should we state it and say we believe it, without somebody charging us with believing man is all right. Man is not all right. Man is a fallen creature. Man went down like an automobile that left the highway at a curve and went over a gully, smashing into the rocks. Man is not all right. Man is lost.

Our salvation is that God created man to know Him. He created man to know Him in a sense and to a degree which no other creature can know God. The creatures that are in the presence of God possibly may not know God as well as the man's soul which God hath made in His image. Do you not see that there has to be a degree of light given which enables a man to know God?

That cat resting under your table, or the dog lying on the rug, would not be moved in the least bit if you were to play either Mozart or Beethoven. He will never open a sleepy eye, because there's nothing in that cat's nature that can understand Beethoven or Mozart. You can put on some fine recordings from London, but no dog will get up and go over and sit down and gaze in wonder even though he knows his master's voice. He can't appreciate it because he hasn't got the kind of light that can appreciate it. But a two-year-old baby will sway its little body, because all babies do that. It's built into them. God put into them the rhythm of the universe. God is the greatest musician in His universe. And so, the little babies are born into the stream of it, just as a fish that's born into the water. And when they're old enough to hear music, they're old enough to smile and sway to it because it's the dance of light that God gave them that kind of nature.

God made us to know Him in a way that no other creature can know Him. He made us to know Him to a degree that no other creature can know Him, because no other creature has quite the capabilities that man has. Certainly, the angels have capabilities; they are holy angels and they obey God. Certainly, the seraphim around the throne shine in the fire of God, and they know God. But they don't know God as man will know God when redemption has been completed. For God means that man should be higher than the angels. God made man a little lower than the angels that He might raise man higher than the angels. And when it's all over and we know as we are known, we shall rank higher in the hierarchy of God than the very angels themselves.

Man, though, by his sin, lost this knowledge. He lost it. We read this in Romans 1, where Paul says even though they knew God, "they glorified him not as God, neither were thankful; but became vain in their imaginations, and their foolish heart was darkened" (Rom. 1:21). Even though they did not want to retain God in their knowledge, God gave them over to a reprobate mind to do those things which were not convenient, as one version says, to do disgraceful acts. Man, because of his sin, lost this knowledge of God. Though he has the potentiality to know God, he still doesn't know God because his conduct is unworthy of his high origin and his heart is filled with a huge emptiness.

And so, that is what's the matter with us. That's why we have these crises all the time. They tell us that science and philosophy and psychiatry and psychology and sociology should make the world a better place in which to live, and all men could all be each other's brothers. But we're hating each other more than ever since the beginning. There's more hatred and more suspicion and more treachery and more spying and more espionage and more selling out than ever there has been since the beginning of the world. What's the matter? It's because man is filled with a vast emptiness. He was created to know God, but because of his sin, he chose the gutter and doesn't want to have God in his knowledge.

What does the Bible teach about sinners not knowing God? First of all, it teaches that God can be known. It teaches that God has not abandoned the human race as He abandoned the angels that sinned. Why did He abandon the angels that sinned? Because they were never made in the image of God in the first place. They were made moral creatures capable of moral and spiritual perception, but they were not made in the image of God. Why did God not abandon man? Because man was made in the image of God, and so God gave man a chance and sent a Redeemer.

How does the Bible teach that man can know God? It teaches we can know God through Jesus Christ, who is the image of the invisible God, the brightness of His glory, and the express image of His person. The church fathers said this about Him: I believe in one Lord Jesus Christ, the only begotten Son of God, begotten in Him before all ages; God of God, light of light, very God of very God, begotten, not made, being of one substance with the Father and by whom all things were made. This is what the Bible teaches. It teaches that everything the Godhead is, Christ is.

Don't listen to the liberals who say God revealed Himself through Christ, and who also say Christ reflected more of God than other people did. Don't listen to them as they say that as one piece of metal might be more radioactive than another, so certain individuals are tuned to God in a way that other individuals aren't, and they are, therefore, religious geniuses. And that Jesus Christ was the supreme religious genius, catching and reflecting more of God than any other man. Don't listen to that, because all that amounts to is an insult to Jesus Christ.

Jesus Christ was not a reflector of Deity only, though He was that. He was not a revealer of Deity only, though He was that. He was and is and always has been and never can cease to be God—Light of light, God of God, very God of very God, begotten and not created. And so, all that the Godhead is, Christ is. To know Jesus Christ is to be back at the Ancient Fountain again.

We have pushed our way on into artificiality so far, but through a wonderful, swift act of our souls in faith and in prayer, we go back to the ancient founding of our being and start over again where we can know God for ourselves all over again, back where Adam started; back beyond where the world began; back beyond where the angels began; back at that ancient, glorious trembling Fountain we call the Being of God, the Triune God. And in Jesus Christ, we go back there.

In Jesus Christ, we leave all the environs and go back to the Ancient Source of our being. Fixed on this blissful center rest. John Newton once wrote: "Now rest, my long-divided heart, fixed on this blissful center, rest." And so, back at the Ancient Source of our being we find the beginnings and start all over in Christ. That I may know Him, said Paul; that I may know Him.

The perplexing question before us is, why do Christians know Christ so little and know God so little? Granted, not all of the Godhead can be known to us. In fact, if you have the idea that you know pretty well all that can be known about God, you're just about to burst. And when you blow, it'll take God a long time to get you back together again. Not all of the Godhead can ever be known, because any being capable of knowing all of the Godhead would have to be equal to the Godhead. Just as you can't pour a quart of water into a vessel holding less than a quart, you can't pour all of the Godhead into an experience of anyone being less than God.

In arguing for the Trinity, the ancient fathers said to look at it like this: God, the Eternal Father, is an infinite God, and His name is love and He is love. In essence, the very nature of love is to give itself, and He could not give His love fully to anybody that was not fully equal to Him. And so therein we have the Ancient Son, who is equal with the Father. And the Eternal Father poured out His love into the Son who could contain it, and contain all of it, because the Son is equal with the Father. And then, said these wise, reasoning old brethren, for the Ancient Father to pour His love out on this Son would mean that a medium of communication had to be there equal to the Father and the Son, and that was the Holy Spirit.

So there you have the Trinity, the Ancient Father in the fullness of His love, pouring Himself through the Holy Spirit who is in being equal to Him, and to the Son, who is in being equal to the Spirit and the Father. So, not all of the Godhead can be known by man, the limitless, infinite sea of being we call God, filling and surrounding and enfolding and upholding. All that can be known of God is revealed in Christ.

When Paul said "that I may know him," he did not mean intellectually. He meant by experience, personally and consciously. He meant that I may know God personally, myself, spirit touching spirit and heart touching heart in conscious knowledge of God. Henry Suso said there is a vast difference between hearing a lute, a sweet lute, sweetly played and merely hearing that one has been played. It is one thing to hear that there's been a concert, and it's another thing to have heard the concert. It's one thing to hear that there has been a planet suddenly discovered, but it's another thing to have gazed on that planet.

This describes a great many Christians. They have heard there's a sweet lute that's been sweetly played, but they've never heard it themselves. They know God only by hearsay. It's my conviction that we tend to know God only by hearsay. Some have never heard of Him except by hearsay, and others have heard Him and have known Him, but only faintly. We've heard only faint echoes of God's voice instead of ever hearing the voice of God. You can always tell a man or a woman who's been into the Presence and come out. There is a vibrancy in their testimony that you don't find anywhere else.

I often claim that I can know much about a place by simply reading about it, but anyone who travels abroad and comes back just smiles when they hear that. If you've actually been there, you know it in a way you can't know if you've only read a book about it. Most Christians have only read a book about God. That's all. They've heard the faint echo of the voice of God. They've seen a reflection of the light of God. They've seen a photograph instead of God Himself, and their personal knowledge of God is very slight.

We often have social fellowship and religious activity and all the various religious props and lean on each other. The Lord Jesus had that. He had His brethren. He had His work to do. He had His healing and raising from the dead and opening eyes and unstopping ears, answering questions and blessing people. He had that. But He also had a personal knowledge of God that was strong and real and individual, so that when He went up into the mountain to pray and waited on God all night, He didn't feel that He was alone. He knew that God was there.

God wants to give you Himself. Isn't it true in the Scriptures that when God creates an order of life, He creates an environment for that life? And when God made man in His image and redeemed him by the blood of the Lamb to bring him back to that image, is not God the environment of the Christian? The great sea we call the ocean is the environment for whales, and the air the environment for birds. The earth is the environment for the nightcrawler and the mole. But the heart of God is the environment for the Christian, and God meant that we should live in that heart of God.

The greatest grief in heaven today is that we want God's gifts but yet don't want God. Even in the church it's the same. If God gives you a rose without giving you God, He's given you a rose with a thorn. And if He gives you a garden without giving you Himself, He's given you a garden with a serpent. And if He gives you wine without giving you God, He's giving you that with which you may destroy yourself.

God wants to give you Himself. We, though, want God for what we can get out of Him. That's the greatest blight that rests upon us. The Sovereign God wants to be loved for Himself, and He wants to be appreciated for Himself. And more than that, He wants us to know that when we have Him, we have all the rest. Jesus said it in another way: "Seek ye first the kingdom of God, and his righteousness; and all these things shall be added unto you" (Matt. 6:33).

Why does God forgive sin? He forgives sin because sin is the shadow that stands between Him and us. If God is ever going to know us and we know God, the shadow has to be removed. So, God forgives sin. Why does God pour out His Spirit on us when we trust Him and believe that He will? It's in order that the Spirit, when He comes, will take the things of God and show them unto you. Why does God answer prayer? In order that in answering prayer, He might unveil His own face to us. Why has God given us the Scriptures? That through the Scriptures we might know God.

The Scriptures, my friend, are not an end in themselves, even though some talk about it as though they were an end in themselves. No man can believe more fully in the verbal inspiration of the Scriptures as originally given than I do. But verbal inspiration or any other theory of inspiration, when it makes the Bible an end in itself, is a dangerous thing. The purpose of the Bible is not to lead you to the Bible. The purpose of the Bible is to lead you to God. The Bible is the lens through which we look and see our Beloved gathering lilies with the dew on His hair, as we read in the Song of Solomon. The Bible is the ladder. The Bible is the means of communication. The Bible is the entrance in. The Bible is never an end in itself.

Oh, that God would raise up somebody that could say this, that could make His church see—the Bible people, the fundamentalists, we evangelicals—that He would raise up somebody that could make us see it. For so long we've undergone indoctrination and brainwashing in a kind of creed that makes God to be our servant instead of us being God's servant. God wants to give gifts, but every gift He gives, He wants to give Himself with His gift. That's the wonder of it. He wants to give Himself.

Nowadays, we use God. We use God to get a job. We use God to give us safety. We use God to give us peace of mind and heaven at last. God, all the while, is searching for those who will say, "God, I don't know, but my heart craves Thee. I want Thee. My heart is in pain, and it can't be at rest until it finds rest in Thee. I'd rather have Thee and nothing than to have everything rolling in my way." Better to have God and a dime than to have all the riches in the world and not have God with it. God is searching for those who will put it all beneath the cloud of forgetting. He doesn't want anybody to stand in and take His place or even remotely take His place. He wants us to seek Him, to seek God.

Somebody once asked John Wesley about seeking God, to which he replied, "If any preacher comes telling you to seek anything more than more love, don't listen to him." The only preaching you ought to listen to is that which says seek more of God. Seek to know the Triune God. You can know all the Godhead revealed in Christ to your soul, infinitely more than you now know. If the church of Christ would only come back to this and get sober-minded and serious and stop fooling and begin to seek for God Himself, then all the gifts of God would come along with God. All the blessings of God would come along with God.

We want the fullness of the Spirit. We want clean hearts. We want a principle within. We want love divine, all loves excelling. We want all of that. But if we seek those things apart from God, we've only found a rose with a thorn. But if we find God, we find all of these things too in God. Better I say a thousand times, know God through Jesus Christ intimately.

But you say, "I have accepted Christ and I'm converted." That's very wonderfully good. But do you know Him? The man Paul had been converted too and was one of the world's greatest Christians when he wrote, "That I may know Him, and the power of his resurrection, and the fellowship of his sufferings, being made conformable unto his death" (Phil. 3:10). He was plowing on and plowing ahead into the knowledge of Jesus Christ, what he called the excellency of the knowledge of Christ Jesus my Lord.

My friend, this is why we were created. Somebody wants to know what the deeper life is. I almost withdraw from the term anymore. I almost shrink from hearing it, because people talk about the deeper spiritual life, but nobody seems to want God. God is the deeper life. Jesus Christ is the deeper life, and as I plunge further into the knowledge of the Triune God, my heart moves out into God further. There's less of me and more of God, and the life becomes deepened and strengthened in God.

Oh, that I might know Him. Anything that keeps me from knowing Him is my enemy. If it is a friend that stands between Him and me, that friend is an enemy. If it is a gift that stands between Him and me, that gift is an enemy. If it is an ambition that stands between Him and me, that ambition is an enemy. If it is a defeat that I once had and I allow that defeat to get me down and stand between Him and me, I'm to forget that; forgetting all the things that are past, I plow on forward and press on. And if it's a victory that I had back there and that victory stands between me and the knowledge of God, I've got to put that victory behind me.

So we can know God for ourselves. Some are finding Him. Some are plowing through. Some are finding the Lord in a new, rich, deep, and wonderful way. Your own longing heart is talking back to you. In the yearning within you there is something bigger than you are. And you may not be quite clear about it intellectually, but your heart cries for God, and you want to know what Paul knew, and you want to know what God has revealed and given to the experience of the saints down through the years. You need to seek God for the spiritual courage and faith to rise and put behind you and under your feet whatever it is—whether friendships or ambitions or hopes or plans or gifts or victories, or anything that prevents you from knowing the Lord Jesus Christ.

11

FREEDOM TO SEE

There has hardly been a time in my ministry when a particular scriptural study has taken more time and given me more pain, as well as requiring more prayer, than the teaching I have been bringing in this book. But because I did and because it was and is so important, I have keenly felt Satan attempting to thwart the purpose of God. It is my belief that he has thwarted the purpose of God in other's lives as well. I have felt as though I have been in raw contact with hell throughout this study on the stages toward completeness in Christ.

There are some things I don't ask God for, that is, that I don't particularly want. There are other things I do ask of Him. One thing I have asked Him in recent years in particular is that I might be in lowercase, if not in capital letters, a lowercase seer. There are so many blind people in the church of Christ that I want to help them see. I want to penetrate and understand and have discernment and know what's going on, and not only know what's going on, but what it means in the whole plan of God. I am not referring to prophecy in particular, although I want to know that too. But I want to be able to appraise the situation and see it as God sees it and know what God thinks of it and know what to do about it and to know the will of God in this present religious confusion.

Having discernment doesn't make a man easy to live with and certainly won't make him popular. It won't fill his church building with people to the point where he has police problems taking care of the crowds. But it does force him sometimes— that is, it has forced me frequently—to follow this trail straight to the Foe. I should hate to think that I could spend my lifetime preaching the Word of God and find that I had never been any- where near the battle line, that I could wear the uniform of the soldiers of Christ and yet have never smelled the burnt powder once in my whole lifetime. And yet, that's possible. It's possible from lack of discernment, from lack of knowledge, from lack of understanding, from lack of prophetic insight, and from lack of the gift of discernment.

It's entirely possible to go through the routine of being a minister of the gospel or a teacher or any kind of gospel worker and never have met the devil once in open combat. I have a few times, and I've sensed it in recent weeks. There is a struggle and combat and wounds and pain. I believe it is the conflict of Jesus being relived in His people, and some of you have felt it too. Because of this study, possibly you have come out into a newer, blessed, happier experience in God which is only begin- ning for you. And possibly, you have felt the conflict and the hot breath that singed your very brow, and you know that you've been where the devil is. I don't like the devil. I don't like to fight. I don't like to pray when you can smell brimstone. I don't like to meet the devil in prayer. But if it's necessary, then God forgive me and help me not to run from it.

We have been examining the stages on the path to Christian maturity in the life of a believer, and I think I have uncovered what is probably the greatest hindrance to our success. Yes, we've heard the voice of Jesus saying, "Lazarus, arise," and we know we're up and out of the grave at least. But why can't we escape from the grave clothes, and why can't we get free? The lack of freedom in the church of Christ is one of the greatest hindrances in the church, this lack of freedom.

I believe our greatest hindrance is the reality of a dark and sinister foe whose name is the devil and Satan, that old dragon, who is busy and dedicated to our damnation despite the fact that he knows there is no use to try to damn a Christian. The devil knows when a child of God is in the hands of God and justification is his. He knows he can't damn him, but he does want to keep his spirit imprisoned. That's the business of the devil. It is to keep either our spirit imprisoned or, changing the figure, if he can't prevent us from being alive, then he keeps us wound up with grave clothes so that we might almost as well be dead. And thus, he robs us of our heritage.

No doubt you, and maybe me to a large degree, are like the sons of a fabulously wealthy man who has died and willed all of his millions to us. And still we go around in rags and with an old stick and poke through the alleys looking for a cast-off crust and sing to our Father in heaven while we munch on the crust with our gums and while a chill wind bites through our ragged clothing and our toes show through our battered shoes. But we're rich nevertheless, as rich as Midas, richer than King Solomon in Christ Jesus. But we're not doing anything about it because Satan is busy, dedicated to keeping us lost. Or if he hasn't succeeded in doing that, if you're a Christian, he can only keep you bound, but not possessed.

Most evangelical Christian teachers today will agree with me that a Christian can't be possessed of evil spirits, but he can be spirit-oppressed and intimidated and silenced and repressed. The work of the devil is to repress and silence. I believe it is perfectly legitimate and entirely scriptural to believe the devil wants to keep us fighting and silenced and intimidated so that if we are alive, we're just barely alive.

Back in the days of the Israelites there was a valley that lay between their warriors and the Philistines. King Saul was leading them, and everybody was scared because an eleven-foot-tall man was going about beating his great, hairy chest and saying, "I defy the army of Israel this day." This continued for some time until a little fellow by the name of David came along. And the Spirit of the Lord came upon the man David. David told Israel, "Let no man's heart fail because of him. Thy servant will go and fight with this Philistine." That was the first encouragement they had there. They were all alive. They were God's people. They were God's soldiers, but they were intimidated so that they couldn't open their mouths as they gazed in fascinated fear at that great giant as he defied them.

I believe any church that wants to make any spiritual progress has got to face this. We are constantly defied by the devil, whether we realize it or not. We Christians need to move from our superficial living and get serious about this and determine that we're going to have all God has for us on earth. Die or live, sink or swim, we're up against raw hell as soon as we name Christ. The devil is not going to let you off easy. I can assure you of this.

There is no question about it, we are a flock of frightened sheep. Jesus Christ came down and took our bodies on Himself. He was a man, very man, born of a woman—a man wearing our nature. And He was also God, and He went out on a cross, and there they sacrificed Him. God Almighty sacrificed Him as the one last, final fulfillment in summation of all the sacrifices that were ever made on Jewish altars. And after He had been three days in the grave, He came out. And after a few days, He ascended through all the barrage of hell to the right hand of God and sat down amidst the acclamations of the heavenly hosts. There He sits at God's right hand, a living man, our representative there. We ought to be the most fearless, the most relaxed, the most utterly self-assured or God-assured people in the wide world, and the happiest people. But we're not, because this devil has intimidated us like old Goliath. "I defy the armies of Israel." What can you do? What are we afraid of?

I believe God has helped me understand what most of us are afraid of. While we could be free, we just can't get free. We just can't be happy Christians. For one, we're afraid of our past sins. Sin is such a terrible thing, and God knows it is and we know it is and the devil knows it is, and he knows how to follow us around, reminding us of our sins. If he can't keep us damned because we're born again, then he keeps us shut up in a little cage. He keeps our wings clipped so we can't fly. We claim we believe that our sins are gone, but we only half believe it. Why do we say that they are gone and then act as if they aren't gone? If they're not gone, why do we say they are? And if they are gone, why do we act as if they are not?

You have been declared not guilty by the highest court in all the wide universe. Therefore, why should you go around frightened? And yet some Christians who wouldn't do a wrong, and deeply want God worse than you want to live, struggle to get loose. The grave clothes trip you up every time you try to run a little faster. Satan uses your past sins to terrify you.

Old Meister Eckhart once said, "God forgives a man and then forgets about his sin and refuses to think of it. When God forgives a man, He trusts him just the same as if he had never sinned." I had never heard anyone say that God trusted people, but old Meister Eckhart, who was a master of the inner life, said when God forgives a man, He doesn't say, "Now, you ought to watch this fellow because he has a bad record." The man now in Christ starts as if he had just been created, as if there had been no past at all.

Another thing that intimidates us is a memory of our failures. Satan will never let you forget it. You've failed and Satan will come and will accuse you of the big to-do you made about the deeper life and being filled with the Spirit and living life in the Spirit, saying, "Look at the flops you've made. Look how many times you've bruised yourself tumbling around." The Bible tells us a man falls seven times, and he rises. The thing isn't that you fail, but if you'll allow it, the devil will chagrin you with that thing.

Did you not know that when God saved you, He knew what kind of a person you were? God Himself in Isaiah 48 said, "Yea, thou heardest not; . . . yea, from that time that thine ear was not opened: for I knew that thou wouldest deal very treacherously, and wast called a transgressor from the womb" (Isa. 48:8). The devil says, "Ah, God doesn't know you like I do. He hasn't watched you as I have. Remember that time? Remember that?"

That's the devil talking. And God says, "I knew that thou wouldest deal very treacherously, and wast called a transgressor from the womb. For my name's sake will I defer mine anger, and for my praise will I refrain for thee, that I cut thee not off. Behold, I have refined thee, but not with silver; I have chosen thee in the furnace of affliction. For mine own sake, even for mine own sake, will I do it" (Isa. 48:8b–11a).

God has a stake in you, Christian, and for His own sake, He'll do it. Don't think He didn't know that you were treacherous. He knows that the blood of Adam runs in your veins and is tainted blood. He knows your nervous system is an Adamic nervous system aggravated by thousands of years of hereditary taint. He knows it and yet says, I knew you were treacherous. I knew you had a heart for it. I knew, but for my own sake, I'm doing this thing. Look away from yourself, friend. God isn't going to bless you for your sake. He's going to bless you for Jesus' sake and for the sake of His own name, for His own glorious name's sake.

If you think there is anyone in the world good enough that God could do anything for their sake, you don't know sin. And if you think there's anything God won't do for you for His sake, you don't know God. Don't let your past failures get you down even though your testimony has been punctured and flattened and spoiled. God knows all about you. You're not responsible to men. You stand responsible before your heavenly Father and Jesus Christ at the right hand of God. So don't let your failures get you down.

Another cause for our lack of freedom is our weaknesses. We all know how weak we are. Thankfully, there are a few who will willingly say, "Lord, Thou knowest my weaknesses. Thou hast noticed all my weaknesses. Thou knowest that when I am weak, then am I strong." And then some of us are frightened sheep because while we stand on the edge of the river, we refuse to go across. We are in Kadesh Barnea, or we're at the Jordan River, and we're afraid to go across because we fear we'll lose our reputation as a sober Christian.

Many cults are willing to be put in jail, cut down, pushed out, and lampooned for the sake of their miserable, twisted doctrine, and we Christians are so concerned about being respectable and smooth. You may be a respectable Christian, but you'll never get where you ought to be until God takes away your respectability—never. You may have a name for being a very sound Christian. We sing Charles Wesley's hymns, but we forget Charles Wesley was considered a donkey by a lot of the sound Christians of his time. We quote Charles G. Finney, but Charles G. Finney was in trouble all the time with the people who stood around and tried to frown him down.

If you go deeper in your walk with God, you'll lose your reputation for a while, but after a while, they'll slowly come back around to you. I lost mine some years back and was even labeled a liberal. I don't know how in the world they could come to that conclusion. They might as well have reported I was Chinese. The report went out I had gone liberal because I stopped talking with the stilted, wooden language of the frightened fundamentalist and began preaching on the deeper spiritual life. Because of that they said I'm a liberal.

There are many who are afraid of fanaticism. Satan will often goad people into violent extremes and fill Christians with a fear of being extreme or a fear of being ostracized. They're afraid because the devil says, "If you go, you'll have to go it alone." The devil is a liar and the father of lies. He's a murderer. He never tells the truth, except he can embarrass you with it. The only truth he ever tells you is to remind you how you've sinned and how you have fallen and the failures you've had and your weaknesses. That's truth, but it is truth used to destroy you.

And then there's a nameless inward chill that I can't quite identify, but it's on the church of Christ. We talk about how happy we are, the shouts of glory, roll the waves of glory, roll the shouts I can't control. We have managed to control them pretty well, haven't we? Many can go to a ballgame and come back hoarse, but seldom does anyone go home from church hoarse. There's a nameless, inward chill that lies like a shadow over our hearts, and that's what we've got. There's no question about it. Examine yourself to see whether you are still under the shadow and wearing the grave clothes. Our Moses has come to deliver us, He who has gone into heaven and is on the right hand of God, angels and authorities and powers being made subject under Him.

We are no longer dealing with a babe in a manger, and we're not dealing with a man on the cross. Formal Christianity deals with a babe in a manger. Catholicism mainly deals with a man on a crucifix, but the Bible tells us there is a Man on a throne, sitting at the right hand of power, and we're dealing with Him. The baby in the manger was weak. The man on the cross was dead, but the Man on the throne is alive forevermore. He carries our names on His shoulders and on His chest and in His hands and wears the holy miter on His forehead.

"Who is he that condemneth? It is Christ that died, yea rather, that is risen again, who is even at the right hand of God, who also maketh intercession for us" (Rom. 8:34). If you were in trouble and you had the best lawyer on the North American continent pleading your cause, don't you think you would sleep better tonight? Remember then, you have the best Advocate above pleading your cause. And we read in Philippians 1:28, "In nothing terrified by your adversaries: which is to them an evident token of perdition, but to you of salvation, and that of God." Ephesians 4:27 says, "Neither give place to the devil." James 4:7 tells us, "Submit yourselves therefore to God. Resist the devil, and he will flee from you."

In the early days of the Christian and Missionary Alliance, the singing wasn't as musical as some choir directors might have liked, but it clearly embodied a risen Savior, the same yesterday, today, and forever. One song was Jesus Is Victor:

> *Jesus is victor! His work is complete,*
> *Crushing all enemies under His feet;*
> *Jesus is victor! He died not in vain,*
> *Risen and glorified, Jesus doth reign.*

> *Jesus is victor! the battle is won,*
> *We can do nothing, for all has been done;*
> *Jesus is victor! the foe from the dust,*
> *Never can rise again, if we but trust.*

And A. B. Simpson wrote:

> *Fainting soldier of the Lord,*
> *Hear His sweet inspiring word:*
> *"I have conquered all thy foes,*
> *I have suffered all thy woes;*
> *Struggling soldier, trust in Me,*
> *I have overcome for thee."*

You don't have to overcome anybody or anything. He's your overcomer.

> *Fear not, though thy foes be strong;*
> *Faint not, though the strife be long,*
> *Trust thy glorious Captain's power,*
> *Watch with Him one little hour;*
> *Hear Him calling, "Follow Me,*
> *I have overcome for thee."*

You have the access and power to overcome through an overcoming Savior. You don't have to do it yourself. You may be trying to do it. You're trying to push and strain and sweat and get through. Ah, my friend, let me tell you, when a priest went into the holy place, they didn't allow him to wear wool. He had to wear linen, because the Bible said they didn't want anybody sweating there before the altar. Human perspiration worketh not the victory of Christ. It took sweat and tears and blood and dying to save us from sin. And it took victorious resurrection and ascension to bring us the victory, but for you and me it just takes trust, trust in the Lord Jesus.

When you get under the load and you begin to get under and you pray and you read the Scripture and you can't get above, and you're under and things are rolling on you, and you're physically down and tired, say to God with a faith imparted from heaven, "Now God, I've had enough of this. I won't take any more. This inner conflict doesn't come from You; this comes from my enemy, the devil, and I'll not take any more of it." When I have prayed this, the burden has rolled away. You don't have to be kicked around. God never meant you to be a football. He meant you to humble yourself and be chastened and let Him do the chastening. But when the devil starts getting funny with you, you dare resist him.

I once walked along a street in an eastern city, heavy with a load on my heart and a burden I couldn't escape, and it was getting bigger. As I walked along the street called Elm Street, I suddenly said, now God, no more of this. I won't take it any longer, and snap, the thing left my heart and I have never had it back on me again. That's not defying God. That's defying the devil and believing God. God loves that kind of courage, my friend. He loves it. It's time we stop letting the devil push us around when we have met every condition we know and we want God worse than we want to live, and we would lie down and die if we knew the Lord wanted us to—God knows it.

It's time for Christians to dare to rise in the sweet faith of the risen Jesus Christ and say, "I will not take this any longer. I'm a child of God! Why should I go mourning all the day?" The burden will roll just as sure as you live. I know from practical experience. I have come up out of tailspins that I think would have put me in the hospital with a nervous breakdown, pressure of work, exhaustion and troubles, and then suddenly I said, now God, I've had enough of this. God in turn says, that's all right, son, I was waiting to hear you say that. I was waiting to hear you say you have had enough. The devil has been kicking you around, and I've just waited to see how long you would take it. And off rolls the burden. So why don't you, poor frightened sheep, just bleat a little in the name of a mighty risen Savior at the right hand of God.

12

COMPLETE IN HIM

My teaching in this study has been based generally on Paul's testimony found in the third chapter of his epistle to the church at Philippi, verses seven through fifteen. Here is what I consider a smooth little translation taken from the Aramaic, the language our Lord and His disciples actually spoke.

So that through this righteousness, I may know Jesus and the power of His resurrection, and be a partaker of His sufferings, even to a death like His; that I may by any means attain the resurrection from the dead. Not as though I had already attained or were already perfect; but I am striving, that I may reach that for which Jesus Christ appointed me. My brethren, I do not consider that I reached the goal; but this one thing I do know, forgetting those things which are behind me, I strive for those things which are before me, I press toward the goal to receive the prize of victory of God's highest calling through Jesus Christ. Therefore let those of you who are perfect think these things over; and if you reason in any other way, God will reveal even that to you. (Phil. 3:10–15, *Holy Bible from the Ancient Eastern Text*)

The apostle Paul says he wasn't perfect. But he said, as many as are, think this over. Throughout the preceding chapters, I have called my readers to come with me to seek the Lord. And my call can be found otherwise worded in Hosea 6:1–3:

> Come, and let us return unto the LORD:
> > for he hath torn, and he will heal us;
> > he hath smitten, and he will bind us up.
> After two days will he revive us:
> > in the third day he will raise us up,
> > and we shall live in his sight.
> Then shall we know, if we follow on to know the LORD:
> > his going forth is prepared as the morning;
> > and he shall come unto us as the rain,
> > as the latter and former rain unto the earth.

Also in Proverbs 4:18 we read, "The path of the just is as the shining light, that shineth more and more unto the perfect day."

For myself, I claim the same testimony as that of Martin Luther. You may remember Luther's prayer: "O Lord Jesus, Thou art my righteousness; I am Thy sin." That's my testimony, "O Lord Jesus, Thou art my righteousness. I am Thy sin." The only sin Jesus ever had was mine, Luther's, and yours. And the only righteousness we can ever have is His. But in spite of the fact that we have been insisting along with Paul, "Not as though

I had already attained, either were already perfect, but I follow after" (Phil. 3:12). The whole gist of my teaching has been this: O Lord Jesus, Thou art my righteousness, but I am Thy sin.

This may sound odd, but it is a delightful thing when you know by experience what the Scripture says—your adversary the devil goes about like a roaring lion, seeking whom he may devour—and then you get close enough to hear him roar. Most Christians, though, never get close enough to the devil, or ever get into lion country. They merely hear that he has roared, but they haven't heard him themselves. All they know is the devil does roar, but they have never been in lion country themselves. All one needs to do is push on deeper in the Christian life and you will get into lion country. For there you'll hear him roar, and he'll be after you. This gears into the whole sweep of the Scriptures.

I want to cap off this teaching on attaining spiritual maturity with a little text which is very lovely to me. It's Hebrews 13:8: "Jesus Christ the same yesterday, and to day, and for ever." I want your eyes to be focused upon Him who never changes. You and I are dealing with the Lord Jesus Christ, after all, and not with doctrines. We're dealing with the Lord of all doctrine. We're dealing with the Source out of which all truth flows—Truth. Doctrine is only truth that's been crystallized so we can get hold of it and come to the Source of all truth: Jesus Christ, the same yesterday, today, and forever. Nothing about Jesus Christ has changed down to this hour. His love hasn't changed nor cooled off. It hasn't increased any because it couldn't. He already loves us with infinite love. You cannot increase infinitude. Nothing about the purpose or interests of Jesus has changed. He's still as interested in the same thing. His purposes are still unchanged. His understanding of us is still the same.

If you give a man money as well as giving him a higher position, he often changes. He may not know it, but he's changed. He gets proud and aloof and unsympathetic. He walks with his head elevated and can't seem to see his old friends. But Jesus Christ our Lord, though He has been raised from the dead and seated at the right hand of the majesty in the heavens and made head over all things to the church and given a name that is above all names, that at the name of Jesus, every knee should bow and every tongue should confess, and though He has been given all authority and power in heaven and in earth, still, He is exactly the same Jesus. He is the same yesterday and today and forever. And even though He has limitless authority and has been made both Lord and Christ, He hasn't changed even one little bit. He's the very same Jesus.

We used to sing a song,

> *Come, sinners, to the Living One,*
> *He's just the same Jesus*
> *As when He raised the widow's son,*
> *The very same Jesus.*

> *Come, tell Him all your griefs and fears,*
> *He's just the same Jesus*
> *As when He shed those loving tears,*
> *The very same Jesus.*

Come unto Him for clearer light,
He's just the same Jesus
As when He gave the blind their sight,
The very same Jesus.

The very same Jesus,
The wonder working Jesus:
O praise His name!
He's just the same.

Jesus Christ is the same now as always, and will be forever.

You are dealing with a Brother who bears your image at the right hand of the Father, who knows all your troubles and your weaknesses and sins and loves you anyway. Jesus stands before the Father being fully responsible for you. He is the Sun that shines upon us. He is the Star of our night. He is the Rock of our hope. He is the Life and the Life-giver. He is our safety and our future. He's our righteousness, our sanctification. He is our inheritance. He's all this, and He's available and He's approachable. And you only have to shut your eyes and in faith move your heart toward Him. The journey to Jesus is not a journey for your feet. It is a journey for your heart. Your feet can be anywhere, but only your heart can make the journey.

I have been following, or at least quoting occasionally from, *The Cloud of Unknowing*, that famous little book that has come down five or six hundred years to us. Its author is unknown, but it is one of the outstanding devotional books of all time. And in that book, as well as many others of that period, they spoke of Mary and Martha and showed how Martha loved Jesus. But her concept of love was activity. She was an active girl. She believed if she loved the Lord, she would be doing something all the time. She was what we call an active Christian. And then Mary, her sister who also loved the Lord Jesus Christ—her concept was quite different. She was fervently occupied in spirit about the love of His Godhead. May we see her as a shining example for us as one who was fervently occupied in spirit for the love of His Godhead.

In today's church, the modern emphasis is upon activity. Do something. We are often like dancing Japanese mice. Have you ever seen them? They call them dancing mice or waltzing mice because they just run continually. Active Christians are on the go all the time, and they feel if they're not attending a church activity or doing something, they are just going nowhere; and around and around they go as fast as water flows, and where she stops nobody knows. Unfortunately, they believe that is spirituality. That was Martha, and we have got a lot of her today.

The Cloud of Unknowing says Mary was fervently occupied in spirit about the love of His Godhead. Oh, I like that. That was another concept altogether. And it was written that Jesus commended Mary and told her one thing is necessary, and Mary has got it. What was that one thing? The old writer said, "It was that God be loved and praised by Himself above all other business, bodily or spiritual, that man may do." That God be loved by Himself. Now, this sounds strange and almost heretical, that God be loved and praised for Himself above all other business, bodily or spiritual, that man may do.

In coming to Jesus Christ, we can be one of two kinds of Christians. We can be an external Christian, the extroverted

Christian who lives outside and neglects his inner life and doesn't know very much about his inner life. You may remember that when Jesus told the disciples to go into all the world and preach the gospel to every creature, Peter jumped up and grabbed his hat and started, and the Lord stopped him and said, not yet, Peter. Don't go like that. Tarry until you are endued with power from on high, and then go.

We, though, want to send them out just as soon as they're born again, just as soon as they get the dust off of the knees from being converted. We give them a handful of tracts and a marked New Testament and say, "Now, get busy." But the Lord never said that. He wants us to learn to worship, and He wants us to have an inner heart experience. He wants us to understand so we have the gift of the Spirit in our hearts that will enable us to do this.

A few years ago in my hearing, the former president of Wheaton College, Dr. J. Oliver Buswell, said the fundamental evangelical church is suffering from a rash of amateurism. He didn't know what a prophet he was when he said that. Today we have religious amateurs running in all directions, forgetting that we are to be occupied with the love of Christ's Godhead and be focused on Jesus Christ and live for Him and be fervently occupied in spirit. We need to love Him and praise Him above all other business, bodily or spiritual—all that man may do in this world—first. Up out of that then grows the profound and lasting and deep and divine activity.

Now it says in *The Cloud of Unknowing* that virtue is not else but an ordained and measured affection plainly directed unto God Himself. Do you want to know what it is to be spiritual? That's it and nothing else. It's nothing else but an ordained and measured affection. That is, it's not a flash of spirituality or emotion. It is more than all that. It is an ordained and measured affection. At the time of that writing six hundred years ago, affection and love were about the same thing—emotion—and it's ordained in measure. It is not pouring itself out like a rainy day and then dry for three more weeks. It's a measured love for the Lord Jesus Christ Himself.

As this book comes to an end, I want to impart some advice. Don't stumble over people in your longing after God and your desire to know Him. Don't stumble over people. People are imperfect. Old Thomas à Kempis in *The Imitation of Christ* said, "If thou wouldst have peace of heart, inquire not too earnestly into other men's matters." If you want to have peace of heart, don't examine your Christian brother too closely, because you'll find things wrong with him. Remember, all idols have clay feet, the imperfections of the saints. That's one thing the devil uses to keep us from going forward, the imperfections of the saints. Don't stumble over them.

Always remember, Jesus Christ is the same yesterday and today and forever, and there's nothing He has ever done for any of His disciples that He will not do for any other of His disciples. Some men who have been considered right-dividers of the Word of truth decided at the turn of the twentieth century that all the gifts of the Spirit were gone and are no longer available to be used anymore, believing they ended when the last apostle died. I wonder where they got that? I'd like to have the chapter and verse on that.

A person can introduce his own ideas into the Scripture while at the same time beat the cover off the Bible and say, "I stand by the Word of God." But what we stand for sometimes is our interpretation of the Word of God handed down from our forefathers by tradition. I find nothing in the Bible that says the Lord has changed in any way. The Lord has never done a thing for any of His disciples that He won't do for any other of His disciples. He's never done anything for any of His disciples that He won't do for you.

He's just the same as He has always been, the same Jesus toward the meek that He has always been. And when the person who is meek comes to Him, He'll never turn him away. His attitude toward the meek is just the same as it always has been. And His attitude toward the mourner—"Blessed are they that mourn: for they shall be comforted"—is the same today as when He spoke those words on the Galilean hillside. His attitude toward the penitential has never changed. The Lord never inquired how deep their sin was. He only inquired as to whether the sinner was sincere and penitential. If he was sorry for his sins and wanted to follow the Lord and repented and turned away from them, the Lord acted as if he had never committed them.

Jesus is the same today toward the honest-hearted person. He's always the same toward those who love Him. Our Lord Jesus Christ doesn't need us. Our God doesn't need us. He's self-sufficient. That's one of His attributes. He does not need us. Before you and I were only dim thoughts in the mind of a planning God before the world was, He was God, and round the throne gathered the seraphim and cherubim and angels and archangels, and principalities and powers, who waved their wings and cried, "Holy, holy, holy is the Lord God Almighty."

What does He need of you, with your breath in your nostrils?

And so, the Lord is always the same toward those who love Him. John leaned his ear against the beating heart of the Son of God, and the Lord loved that. John was called the disciple whom Jesus loved. Not that the Lord didn't love the rest, but He couldn't love them as much because they didn't reciprocate as much. But you and I will find Him just the same. And you'll find Him the same toward those who seek His company, people who seek Him and want to be with Him. They want to be with Jesus. He wants those who are occupied with the love of His Godhead and who seek His company.

He is the same Jesus toward the ignorant and the troubled. Many are ignorant and troubled these days and too often seek help from worldly counselors. I can tell you, though, where you can go to find one who understands you and knows all about you. He didn't learn it from Freud. He didn't get it from Jung, or any of the psychologists. He knew all about you before you were born. And He's the same yesterday, today, and forever. So, if you come to Him knowing something, you will find a very cold reception. But if you come to Him admitting you know nothing, you'll find Him the sweetest teacher in the world. If you come to Him troubled, He is the One who helps the troubled heart. So, we will find Jesus Christ.

To sum up this study, it all comes down to this: all you need is Jesus Christ, the Son of God. He is God and man. He is God and He is man. He is all that a guilty sinner needs, and He is all that the loftiest saint can ever hope. You can never go beyond Him. There's never such a thing as having Him teach you all He can teach you. No, no, He'll be your teacher while the world stands because He's infinite and He is God. You will never know enough to hope that you can ever graduate. The Lord never gives diplomas. I'm so glad for that. He never gives degrees and says, "Inasmuch as you did this and that . . . we confer on you." He'll never do that.

The apostle Paul never got his degree, for he said, "Not as though I had already attained." Paul was in the college of life studying with the Lord Jesus Christ, having no righteousness of his own, pressing forward. His study wasn't the ivory tower study, reading it out of a book and taking notes. It was in tears and pain and suffering and rebuff and persecution and tribulation and trouble and woe. It was all of that and still he said, "I follow after, if that I may apprehend that for which also I am apprehended."

You say, maybe Paul did get his degree because he said he had finished his course. When the time came, he could say, I have attained, I've fought the fight, I've kept the faith, I've run the race. Then the Lord let him bow his beloved neck and the Roman sword whistled down and brought the end to that mighty life that we know as the apostle Paul. And yet, did it bring an end to his life? No, for he said, "he is able to keep that which I have committed," and what he had committed was that very life. You could say he was in the left hand of Jesus, and when the sword whistled down, he passed into the right hand of Jesus—but one thing for sure, he never passed out of the hands of Jesus.

I can only say along with John, "Behold the Lamb of God." Have complete faith in Him. Look now forward and let be backward. Think not of the past. Don't stumble over people, over preachers, over teachers, over our ignorance, over our faults. Don't let anybody praise you to death, and don't let anybody blame you to death. Remember that the holiest man that ever walked the streets of Jerusalem was once called a devil. Remember that.

Don't let anyone blame you and stop you. Just press on. You will find Him to be the very, very same Jesus as when He went away. Come unto Him for clearer light. He's just the same Jesus as when He gave the blind their sight. The very same Jesus. All you need is more of Jesus, and you can have more of Him. And you can have experiences with Him that will be transforming in their intensity and scope and power, if you'll only believe it.

A PRAYER

O our Savior, as we bring this study to an end, we're not bringing to an end our thirst, our determination, our purpose, but we are pressing on. We've got the hilltop in view. And that without any righteousness of our own, but having only that righteousness which is of God by faith, we press forward toward the prize. We thank Thee, Lord God, that there are experiences of power and of liberation and of deliverance. There is a passing out of Egypt and the passing across the Jordan into the Holy Land and moving up and moving in, and the driving out of the inhabitants and the taking over. All these are before us. We pray that Thou would put a quiet but steadfast purpose within our hearts that we may seek Thy face, determined that whatever the cost, we will serve Thee.

We pray, our Lord Jesus, that Thou wilt put the right books into the hands of the hungry-hearted and get them aimed in the right direction and let light fall upon the Word. Bring truth to sight. Save us, we beseech Thee, from the tradition of the elders. And may we, with a burst of spiritual imagination and aspiration and longing, leap forward as the church gets cooler and colder and religion gets further and further from New Testament standards, that we may set our hearts like a flint, determined that we're going to be as Lot in Sodom, as Daniel in Babylon, as the saints in Caesar's household, and as all of those have had to be—to live above our environment and live above our religious environment and take our stand above it and rest in Thee. Gracious Father, grant this, we beseech Thee. This we ask in the name of Jesus our Lord. Amen.

SOURCES

A sermon series preached by A. W. Tozer at Southside Alliance Church in Chicago, Illinois, January–March 1957. Transcribed from original audio tapes.

Chapter 1: "Considering Perfection in the Christian Life," January 13, 1957

Chapter 2: "Four Kinds of Christians," January 20, 1957

Chapter 3: "The Special Christian," January 27, 1957

Chapter 4: "Discovering the Loveliness of Jesus Christ," February 3, 1957

Chapter 5: "Knowing Christ in His Fullness," February 10, 1957

Chapter 6: "The Will of God and Its Relationship to Our Cross," February 17, 1957

Chapter 7: "Seeking God and Finding Him," February 24, 1957

Chapter 8: "Clouds of Concealment," March 3, 1957

Chapter 9: "The Obstacle of Self Trust," March 10, 1957

Chapter 10: "That We May Know Him," March 17, 1957

Chapter 11: "The Church's Lack of Freedom," March 24, 1957

Chapter 12: "Living in His Righteousness," March 31, 1957

Tozer's bestseller, this book has been called "one of the all-time most inspirational books" by a panel of Christian magazine writers.

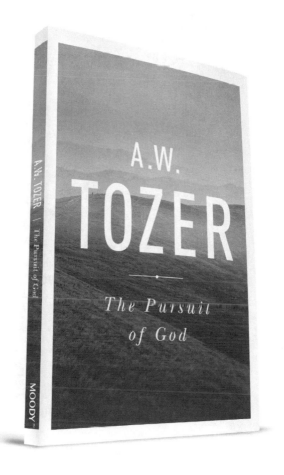

The Pursuit of God is a Christian classic about reclaiming God's presence in a clamoring world. Bringing the mystics to bear on modern spirituality, A. W. Tozer raises high our thoughts of God, makes low our love for the world, and draws our gaze to the heights of heaven.

978-1-60066-003-0 | also available as an eBook

Encounter God. Worship more.

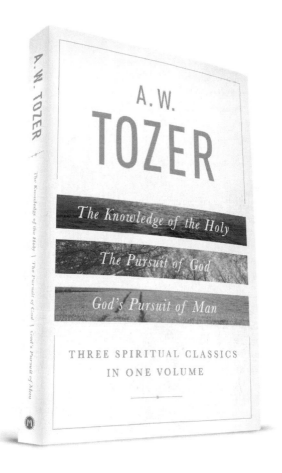